Short Instruction
On True Christianity

for young and simple people to be used in the home and schools

Composed from the Divine Word

by

Nicolaus Hunnius, Doctor.
Superintendent in Lübeck.

Wittenberg / A.D. 1696

Repristination Press
Malone, Texas

Original Title: *Kurze Anweisung Zum Wahren Christenthumb für junge und einfältige Leute im Haus und Schulen zu gebrauchen: Aus Göttlichem Wort gestellt durch NICOLAUM HUNNIUM, Doct. Superintendenten zu Lübeck.*(Wittenberg, Anno 1696). Translation © 2024 by Repristination Press. All rights reserved by Repristination Press. No part of this publication may be reproduced, stored in a retrieval system, or transmitted in any form or by any means, electronic, mechanical, photocopying or otherwise without the prior written permission of Repristination Press.

First edition, November 2024.

REPRISTINATION PRESS
716 HCR 3424 E
MALONE, TEXAS 76660

www.repristinationpress.com

ISBN (10) 1-891469-86-x
ISBN (13) 9781891469862

Table of Contents

4

Foreword to the English Translation.

It is a joy to publish another volume from the works of Nicolaus Hunnius (1585–1643). Like his father, Aegidius (1550–1603), Nicolaus has not received as much attention in the modern revival of interest in the theologians of the Age of Lutheran Orthodoxy (1580–1713). The neglect of the writings of Nicolaus Hunnius is particularly unfortunate, since even the theologians of the 19th century (e.g., C.F.W. Walther) recognized that the writings of this faithful father are of profound importance.

Hunnius' various writings demonstrate a capacity for explaining and defending the faith in a wide variety of contexts. Some of his works, such as the *Diaskepsis Theologica* (1626), are among the most challenging available to a modern audience. Others, such as his *Epitome Credendorum*, were intended for a lay audience.

Hunnius' *Kurze Anweisung Zum Wahren Christenthumb ...* (1637) is intended for a lay audience; indeed, he wrote it for the instruction of children. While it might be tempting to see Hunnius' *Short Instruction on True Christianity* as "just another explanation of the Small Catechism," even a casual perusal of the text will quickly disabuse the reader of any such notion. Hunnius was all too familiar with the burgeoning roster of such works, and his *Short Instruction...* was deliberately intended to be something more holistic when it came to teaching the faith. Hunnius asks in his first question, "In what does the whole of Christianity consist?," and provides this answer: "In three parts: (1) In Christian faith, (2) in a godly life, and (3) in a blessed death." The entirety of this work is built on this tripartite understanding of Christianity. While Pietists would later claim that orthodox Lutherans had little concerning for the godly life, works such as Hunnius' *Short Instruction...* refute such a claim. Like his father before him, Nicolaus Hunnius was quite concerned for the inculcation of a Christian piety which found belief in the Christian verity expressed in a godly life and preparation for a godly death.

It is our hope that this English translation will allow pastors, teachers, and parents access to this resource as its author intended: as a supplement in the formation of catechumens of all ages. As Hunnius knew all too well, it is never too early for the faithful to prepare for a godly death. And the daily exercise of godliness—an emphasis which Hunnius shared with his contemporary, Johann Gerhard (1582–1637)—is the calling of all those who have been baptized into Christ.

Rt. Rev. James D. Heiser, M.Div., S.T.M.
Bishop, the ELDoNA
Pastor, Salem Lutheran Church (Malone, Texas)
Festival of St. Martin of Tours, Bishop and Confessor, A.D. 2024

Preface.

Reminder to all who will use this instruction.

By means of Christian teaching in the old apostolic churches, the peoples recognized the manifold errors and devilish pagan idolatry and turned away from it toward Christianity, but they were not immediately simply accepted into the Christian faith; instead, they were also provided with necessary instruction in the churches and guided to the use of the Holy Sacrament of the Lord's Supper. Moreover, they also later required further instruction, and those churches again strengthened their brothers, as the holy Paul reports, when he writes in 1 Cor. 3: "Paul planted, Apollos watered, etc." Also, one found at those places where the blessed Word had been accepted, the first confirmation, through which the planted doctrine was further advanced and strengthened in the hearts. Furthermore, for better introduction of this blessed work, public catechism instruction was established in the churches, so that a teacher would call together, at a certain time, those who had not yet been introduced into Christianity and guide them, little by little, through question and answer to the knowledge of the necessary doctrinal points. And when they had received this assigned instruction, they were allowed to partake of the Holy Communion.

But since the useful addition with time was made into a sacrament, which in the Papacy was called Confirmation, [it] became a vain show and useless ceremonies were introduced, and thereby the catechism was discarded in the Roman Church and the people were almost brought down into similar darkness. Yet God, through His great mercy, and through the blessed services of Dr. Martin Luther, led [people] out of the dark Papacy to His eternal light of knowledge, and at the same time gave the catechism as a teaching tool from Scripture for children and the simple-minded, through which countless people have come to the true Christian faith, to a holy life, and to eternal salvation: For which unspeakable blessings of His divine grace, eternal praise, honor, glory, and thanks be given!

Since love for the truth has, for some time, diminished among others and is almost growing very cold, many kindhearted and learned men have been moved to encourage people by bringing forth their Christian and useful thoughts in a manner helpful for the exposition of the Catechism, and have explained it so abundantly that the saving doctrine has prompted people to eagerly draw from it for themselves and their households. They have been able to resolve even the most minute doubts, but also to encourage greater diligence and earnestness. Home teachers have compiled small and concise systems, following the same Catechism instruction, though in somewhat different order, to present to the youth. However, those who engage with it reveal another deficiency, as they almost exclusively instruct the youth in doctrine alone, but concerning godliness and how one should prepare for the blessed end, they either give no report at all or a very brief one.

Thus, after I, for special reasons, had undertaken to compose a guide to Christianity for the youth, I should therefore take care not to neglect including the doctrine that already concisely and understandably summarizes everything in a Christian and simple manner, and also to conclude it with instructive reflections on death and with work that serves this purpose. For upon these three points[1] rests the entirety of Christianity.

Up to now, a twofold great deficiency has been found in the Catechism and other holy writings which must be addressed: *First,* that some have taught from superficial and merely human opinions and have not understood the true and proper meaning. This has come about because parents at home and teachers in schools have been content when the children have learned empty words without any understanding and knew nothing else to recite, like a nun with her Latin psalter or a parrot that repeats the words it has been taught. With this method of teaching, they served the little ones poorly, and those who fancied themselves to possess much knowledge deceived themselves with a miserable illusion.

---

1 i.e., doctrine, godliness, and a blessed end.

But since neither the Catechism nor other Christian instruction have been written so that one should merely babble some empty words, but rather that one should learn to grasp with good understanding the teachings contained within, therefore, I hereby most diligently exhort and request everyone—young and old, parents, teachers, and whoever might wish to make use of this humble work of mine—to be very careful to ensure that it is not merely the *mouths* and *lips* of the simple people being taught, but that their *hearts* may be instructed, and that they may be led to a proper *understanding* in these matters. I consider it very helpful if the questions are not fixed solely on the words set forth here, and if the youth are encouraged to use other words in their answers, and that one would not rest until it is clearly perceived that they have grasped the content and the teachings contained within with proper understanding, so that they can give a good answer to anyone, no matter in what form the questions are presented.

Second, the teaching of the Catechism is also a great marvel, when one explains a matter thoroughly to children or the simple-minded, so that they learn to grasp it correctly and precisely, and do not leave without understanding it, as if one had given them wings to fly over hot coals. When the entire book is read from beginning to end, no one knows anything about it afterward, and such instruction must be read ten times fluently before understanding and memory are fully established, because it would otherwise be impossible to grasp it properly.

Thus, this method will not waste time and effort in vain. Therefore, I must immediately exhort and request that parents and teachers take it upon themselves with diligence and earnestness to repeat, rehearse, drive into, and instill in the youth as often and as much as necessary, until it can be hoped that they will never forget it all their lives. Only then, and not before, should they proceed to the next chapter. Then, from time to time, take an hour to review and repeat what was taught previously, so that it does not slip from their memory.

Do not doubt that if this method is followed, and with sincere godliness and devout prayer to GOD, who teaches us what is useful, the dear youth will be rightly and healthily guided to true Christianity. May the Almighty, through the grace of His Holy Spirit, grant heavenly blessing and the desired success! Amen. Written in Lübeck, June 9th, 1637.

NICOLAUS HUNNIUS,
Doctor of Theology, Superintendent there.

Simple Instruction on How to Lead the Youth to True Christianity.

The First Part of the Christian Faith.

1. Summary of Christianity.

1. In what does the whole of Christianity consist?
In three parts: (1) In Christian faith, (2) in a godly life, and (3) in a blessed death.

2. What does the Christian faith teach?
The Christian faith teaches me to place a firm trust in God, that He (though I am a sinful person and not worthy of His grace), will, for the sake of Christ's merit, be merciful to me, forgive my sins, and make me a partaker of eternal life and salvation.

2. Concerning GOD.

3. Since God is the foundation of faith, tell me, what is God?
God is a spirit, eternal, almighty, all-knowing, omnipresent, truthful, merciful, holy, and just, who created everything from nothing, both the visible and the invisible.

4. What do you mean when you say that God is a spirit?
Since Christ says in *John 4*, "God is a spirit," and His spirit has neither flesh nor bones, as stated in *Luke 24*, therefore, God is a spirit because He has neither flesh nor bones; His eternal divine essence does not possess flesh, like human flesh, nor bones.

5. How is God eternal?
In that He has neither beginning nor end, as the 90th Psalm says: "Before the mountains were born, or You brought forth the earth and the world, from everlasting to everlasting, You are God."

6. Why do you call God almighty?

Because God can do exceedingly beyond all that we ask or think, as said in *Ephesians 3*, and He does all that He wills, as stated in *Psalm 115*. Therefore, He calls Himself the Almighty God in *Genesis 17*.

7. What is God's omniscience?

That God examines hearts and minds, as stated in *Psalm 7*, and understands the thoughts of man from afar, as stated in *Psalm 139*.

8. Is God present in all places of the world?

Yes, for He fills heaven and earth, *Jeremiah 23*. The heavens, even the highest heavens, cannot contain Him, *1 Kings 8*.

9. What is to be understood concerning God's truthfulness?

That God is truthful, and what He promises, He surely fulfills, *Psalm 33*. The Strength of Israel does not lie or change His mind, for He is not a man, that He should regret anything, *1 Samuel 15*.

10. How is God merciful?

In that He does not cast us sinners, who deserve His punishment, away in anger, but has mercy on us, subdues our sins, and casts them into the depths of the sea, *Micah 7*. So that we do not have to die: The goodness of the Lord is that we are not consumed; His mercies never end, but are new every morning, and His faithfulness is great, *Lamentations 3*.

11. What do you understand by God's holiness?

That nothing sinful or evil is in Him, *Deuteronomy 32*. Therefore, He alone is holy, *1 Samuel 2*, and He wants us not to defile ourselves with sin, but to be holy, as He is holy, *Leviticus 11*.

12. In what does God's righteousness consist?

In this: (1) His words and order are just; (2) He Himself governs all things in righteousness and wisdom; (3) A sinner does not please the Him, *Psalm 5:1, 4*. He judges all the works of men so that each one may receive what he has done in the body, whether good or bad, *2 Corinthians 5.*

13. How many Gods are there?

There is only one God, *Deuteronomy 6:* "Hear, O Israel: The Lord your God is one Lord." And *Isaiah 44*, "I am the First and the Last, and apart from Me there is no God." So also testifies St. Paul, *1 Corinthians 8*, "We have only one God."

14. If there is only one God, how is it that we call upon and honor not only God the Father, but also the Son and the Holy Spirit as God?

There is only one God; but in the one God, there are three Persons: the Father, the Son, and the Holy Spirit. *1 John 5:* "There are three that bear witness in heaven: the Father, the Word, and the Holy Spirit; and these three are one." Since we are baptized only in God's name, *1 Peter 3*, yet in the name of the Father, Son, and Holy Spirit, *Matthew 28*, the three Persons must indeed be the one God.

15. Can you confirm this even more firmly?

Yes, indeed: The heavenly Father is truly God, which no one doubts. However, Christ the Son is also that same God, as is the Holy Spirit. Therefore, without a doubt, there are three Persons, each of whom is the one true divinity.

3. Concerning Christ's Divinity.

16. Prove that the Son of God is true God.

This is proven by:

(1) The divine names: That Christ is called the blessed God forever, *Romans 9*, the only Lord, *1 Corinthians 8*, the Lord from heaven, *1 Corinthians 15*, the Lord of glory, *1 Corinthians 2*, the Lord of lords, *Revelation 19.*

(2) The divine attributes: That He is eternal, *Micah 5*, His origin is from ancient times, from the days of eternity. Almighty, *Hebrews 1*, He upholds all things by His powerful word. All-knowing,

John 2, He knows well what is in man. Therefore, St. Peter says to Christ, *John 21*, "Lord, you know all things."

(3) Divine works: Creation, *John 1*, "All things were made through the Word, and without Him nothing was made that has been made." The preservation and governance of all creatures, *Hebrews 1*, "The Son upholds all things by His powerful word." The miracles, *Mark 16*, "Christ confirmed the apostles' word with the accompanying signs."

(4) Divine honor, *John 5*, "The Father has entrusted all judgment to the Son, so that they may honor the Son as they honor the Father." Hebrews 1, "Let all God's angels worship Him."

4. Concerning the Divinity of the Holy Spirit.

17. How do you know that the Holy Spirit is true God?

From the same causes:

(1) Divine names: He is called God, *Acts 5*: "Why has Satan filled your heart to lie to the Holy Spirit? You have not lied to men but to God."

(2) Divine attributes: Omniscience, *1 Corinthians 2*: "The Spirit of God searches all things, even the depths of God." Omnipresence, *Psalm 139*: "Where shall I flee from your Spirit? And where shall I flee from your presence?"

(3) Divine works: Creation, *Psalm 33*: "The heavens were made by the word of the Lord, and all their host by the breath of His mouth." The governance of the Christian churches. *Acts 20*: "The Holy Spirit has appointed you as bishops[2] to shepherd the congregation of God." The prophecy of divine matters. *2 Peter 1*: "Holy men of God have spoken, led by the Holy Spirit." The Christian life: "God saves us through the washing of regeneration and renewal by the Holy Spirit," *Tit. 3*.

5. Concerning Creation.

18. Are heaven, earth, and other creatures also from eternity, as eternal as God is?

2 *Bischöfen.*

No. "In the beginning, God created heaven and earth," *Genesis 1*. God says, *Isaiah 44*: "I am the Lord who does all things, who alone stretches out the heavens, and who spreads out the earth without help."

19. Was there anything before, out of which God made everything?

Nothing. It is written in *Hebrews 11*, "Everything that is seen has been made out of nothing." And in *Romans 4*, "The Lord calls into existence the things that do not exist, that they may be."

20. What moved God to create the creatures?

He made everything for His own sake, *Proverbs 16*, so that His eternal power and divinity may be recognized in the creation of the world, *Romans 1*, and in the great beauty and works of this creation's Creator, as in a reflection, *Wisdom 13:5*.

21. Which creatures should recognize God's glory?

The rational creatures, which are in heaven and on earth; namely, angels and humans.

6. Concerning the Angels.

22. What do you understand by the word "angel"?

I understand it to mean a rational creature which has neither flesh nor bones and whose office is to serve God continually.

23. Explain this to me from Holy Scripture?

The angels are spirits, *Hebrews 1*, and invisible creatures, *Colossians 1:16*. They are rational beings, as God's servants, who carry out His commands. These are His hosts, the mighty heroes who do His bidding, *Psalm 103*.

24. Are they so mighty that they are called strong helpers, and so numerous that they are called hosts?

Because of their power and strength, they are called mighty ones, *Colossians 1:16*. And they have a great host who carry out

His commands, *Psalm 103*. Their number is many thousands upon thousands, *Daniel 7, Revelation 5*.

25. Is there a distinction among the angels?

Yes, for there are evil and good angels. The evil ones were created holy and good by God, but they have fallen away from Him and have become His irreconcilable enemies, so that Christ has no harmony with Belial, *2 Corinthians 6*. They are also fierce enemies of humanity, as they are called the old dragon, *Revelation 9*, a murderer from the beginning, *John 8*, roaring lions seeking to devour us, *1 Peter 5*. Therefore, all Christians renounce the devil and his works in Baptism.

7. Concerning the Creation of Man and God's Image.

26. Are humans also created by God?

Yes. In the beginning, God created only one man, Adam, and from his blood He populated the entire earth, *Acts 17*. However, they were originally created without sin, in the image of God.

27. What is God's image?

The divine image is a perfection of human nature that is pleasing to God, which consists of: (1) the knowledge of God and His creatures, (2) complete righteousness, (3) immortal holiness, (4) free will to do good and avoid evil, (5) in submission to God's dominion over physical creatures, (6) in purity and truth of heart, (7) in perfect love for God and neighbor.

28. Since I hear that God's image consists of seven distinct parts, explain these individually.

(1) The knowledge of God: Just as no one knows what is in God except the Spirit of God, *1 Corinthians 2*, so too was man on earth like God, in that he knew God, *Colossians 3*. "Put on the new self, which is being renewed in knowledge after the image of Him who created him."

(2) Knowledge of creatures: Just as God knows all creatures, so Adam knew the names of all animals, *Genesis 2*. He saw

his Eve at first glance as God had made her, that she was of his own flesh, *Genesis 2.*

(3) Complete righteousness and holiness: "Put on the new man, which after God is created in true righteousness and holiness," *Ephesians 4.*

(4) Free will to do good and avoid evil: *Sirach 15:14,* "God created man from the beginning and gave him the choice; if you keep the right sense, you will be given fire and water; take whichever you want: man has before him life and death, whichever he chooses will be given to him."

(5) Immortality: Just as God alone is immortal, *1 Timothy 6,* so He created man for eternal life and made him in His image so that he should be like Him.

(6) Dominion over creatures: Just as the earth belongs to the Lord, *Psalm 24,* so God also gave man dominion over His creatures, *Genesis 1:* "Let us make man in our image, that he may rule over the fish in the sea, over the birds in the sky, over the livestock, and over the whole earth, and over all the creatures that move along the ground."

8. Of the Fall of Man.

29. How does it happen that these acquired gifts are not found in us?

The reason is that man fell into sin when he ate from the tree of the knowledge of good and evil, against God's command, *Genesis 3.*

30. Has he thereby lost all the aforementioned gifts of the Divine Image?

Yes, all of them, for we sinful humans lack:

(1) The knowledge of God, *1 Corinthians 2:* "The natural man does not understand the things of the Spirit of God; they are foolishness to him, and he cannot perceive them."

(2) The knowledge of creatures, *Wisdom 9:* "We barely recognize what is on earth, and we find it difficult to discover what is present."

(3) (4)[3] Complete righteousness and holiness, *Genesis 6*: "All the imagination and thoughts of man's heart are only evil continually." *Isaiah 64*: "We are all like the unclean, and all our righteousness is like a filthy garment."

(5) Free will to do good and avoid evil, *John 8*: "Whoever commits sin is a slave to sin." *Romans 7:21*: "We are slaves to sin, in the law of sin."

(6) Immortality, *Romans 5*: "Through one man's sin, sin came into the world, and through sin, death; and so death passed to all men."

(7) Dominion over earthly creatures: The animals, due to sin, are disobedient and harmful to man, as experience shows. The Israelites were killed by serpents, *Numbers 21*. The Samaritans by lions, *2 Kings 17*.

31. But if the first people sinned, should all their descendants be punished for their sin?

No one is punished for the sin of their parents. However, because the first parents became sinful, they also begot sinful children and brought the evil nature upon their descendants, all of whom, from birth, bear original sin in themselves.

9. Concerning Original Sin.

32. What is original sin?

Original sin is the corruption of nature, through which a person is inclined away from God, from His will and works, and is unable to do them as God wishes, but rather opposes them with full force, and does evil with desire and joy.

33. So original sin is in all humans?

Yes, in all people (except Christ). For all children learn and do evil of their own accord, with delight and joy, but they hate the good and only learn it with compulsion and reluctance. Each person

---

3 Points 3 and 4 are combined. Other editions were consulted to verify this and the text was consistent.

finds this in himself: when he is to pray, read, or hear God's Word, it feels tedious and wearisome, even for a short time, with useful work seeming difficult. But when it comes to walking, drawing, playing, dancing, etc., time always seems too short. This is an innate sinful nature, the fruit and unmistakable signs of it.

34. Does God's Word teach this?

Yes: (1) We are tainted with sin and have inherited sinful parents. *Job 15:* "What is a man, that he should be pure, and that he should be righteous, who is born of a woman? Behold, among His saints, there is not one without fault, and the heavens are not pure before Him; how much less a man, who is vile and corrupt, who drinks injustice like water." (2) All men have become sinners through the fall of one man. *Romans 5:* "Through the sin of one sinner, all corruption has come." (3) All men must lament with David, *Psalm 51:* "Behold, I was conceived in iniquity, and my mother conceived me in sin."

35. What are the effects and fruits of original sin in humans?

(1) Corruption of nature: 1. In their understanding, such that divine mysteries are foolishness to them, and they cannot comprehend it, *1 Corinthians 2.* The crucified Christ is a stumbling block to the Jews, foolishness to the Greeks. *1 Corinthians 1.* 2. In their will, such that all their desires and inclinations are evil continually, *Genesis 6.* Therefore, the will is not free for the good, but is captive under sin, *Romans 7.*

(2) Actual sins: *Matthew 15:* "Out of the heart come evil thoughts, murder, adultery, fornication," etc.

(3) God's Wrath: *Ephesians 2:* We were by nature children of wrath.

(4) Temporal fate: *Romans 6:* "The wages of sin is death." *Romans 5:* Death reigns also over those who have not sinned with the same transgression as Adam.

(5) Exclusion from God's Kingdom: *1 Corinthians 15:* Flesh and blood cannot inherit the kingdom of God.

10. Concerning actual sin.

36. If man has such an evil nature, will he undoubtedly commit many sins daily?

Certainly, there are no humans without daily sins, for whatever man undertakes, the flesh always adds something impure to it, *Sirach 27.* Therefore, St. Paul laments: "The good that I will to do, I do not do, but the evil that I do not will to do, I do," *Romans 7.*

37. How can I know what sin is?

From the Law or the Ten Commandments, *Romans 3.* I recognize sin through the Law. Thus, I would not have knowledge of sin without the Law. All sin is what goes against the divine Law, *John 3.* This includes even a bad word, gesture, or thought.

38. Is it then also a sin if a person unknowingly acts against the Ten Commandments?

Yes, certainly. Therefore, David prays in *Psalm 19*, "Who can understand his errors? Forgive me my hidden faults." St. Paul writes about himself that he unknowingly sinned, *1 Timothy 1*, and yet lived in unbelief.

39. Do you also count evil thoughts among sins?

Certainly: (1) For evil thoughts are also forbidden in the law: "You shall not covet." (2) Evil desire is expressly called sin. *Romans 7*: "I would not have known sin except through the law: for I would not have known what coveting was, if the law had not said, 'You shall not covet.'" (3) Evil desires wage war against the soul, *1 Peter 2*, therefore, they are sin.

40. Do all people sin without exception?

Yes, and children are not excluded either, for the desires and inclinations of the human heart are only evil continually from youth onward, *Genesis 6 and 8.*

41. Perhaps holy, reborn people will be without sin?

No, not even they. For (1) all the saints must ask God for

the forgiveness of their sins, *Psalm 19*, that He may forgive them their hidden faults, *Psalm 32*. (2) All people are saved solely through Christ's merit, *Acts 15*. Only through Christ are sins forgiven and people saved, *Matthew 9*.

42. What are the causes of sin?

The devil is the first cause of sin. *1 John 3*, "Whoever commits sin is of the devil, for the devil has sinned from the beginning." After that, all kinds of sins come from our own flesh, which is corrupted by original sin, *Matthew 15*, "Out of the heart come evil thoughts, murder, adultery," etc.

43. Is God not at all the cause of sin?

No. "You are not a God who delights in wickedness," *Psalm 5*. God is holy and just, and He wills no one to sin.

44. Are all sins the same, or do they differ?

All sins are the same in that even the smallest sin deserves eternal punishment, *Deuteronomy 27*: "Cursed is he who does not uphold all the words of this law." However, sins do have their distinctions otherwise.

45. What is the difference?

(1) Mortal sins are against the love of God and against the love of one's neighbor.

(2) Mortal sins are deadly sins and happen out of malice; daily sins are everyday sins and happen out of natural weakness, even without going against the will.

(3) Mortal sins can be forgiven, while others have no forgiveness.

11. Concerning the sin against the Holy Spirit.

46. Cannot all sins be forgiven?

Our Lord Christ says in *Matthew 12*, "Whoever speaks against the Holy Spirit, it will not be forgiven, neither in this world nor in the world to come."

47. What kind of sin is this?

It is a willful, persistent denial and blasphemy of the saving truth that is known; namely, the gracious forgiveness of sins through Christ. However, those who insult the saving doctrine out of ignorance, like St. Paul in *1 Timothy 1*, or out of fear of persecutors, like Peter in *Matthew 26*, do not sin against the Holy Spirit.

48. Why is this sin not forgiven?

It is not due to a lack of God's will, for where sin increased, God's grace abounded all the more, *Romans 5*. Nor is it due to a lack of Christ's merit, for the blood of Jesus Christ cleanses us from all sin, *1 John 1*. That is why Christ says in *John 6*: "Whoever comes to Me, I will never cast out." Rather, it is because such a person neither desires grace nor the merit of Christ and already tramples them underfoot. He listens neither to the Law nor the Gospel, rejects the ministry of preaching, and deprives himself of all means of repentance and forgiveness of sins. This is why this sin cannot be forgiven.

49. What common fruits do sins produce?

(1) God's wrath. *Romans 1*: The wrath of God is revealed from heaven against all ungodliness and unrighteousness of men.

(2) A guilty conscience. *Wisdom 17*: The heart that is dismayed—its own wickedness causes it, which convicts and condemns it.

(3) Eternal hellish damnation. *Revelation 21*: The fearful and unbelieving, and abominable, and murderers, and whoremongers, and sorcerers, and idolaters, and all liars will have their part in the lake which burns with fire and brimstone.

50. How can a man be helped so that he does not perish in sin?

Only through God's mercy. For no one can help himself, nor can any man help another, *Psalm 49*: "No man can by any means redeem his brother, nor give to God a ransom for him, for the redemption of their soul is costly, and it must be left alone forever." God's justice does not allow the sinner to go unpunished, for His wrath has no end, *Sirach 5*, and it burns to the lowest hell, *Deuteronomy 32*. Thus, God's mercy has no place unless atonement is made for the sinner.

12. Concerning the Law.

51. If this is so, why did God give the Law to man, if it concerns His justice?

The divine Law is God's ordinance according to which, as with a rule, men should govern their entire life and all their actions, and it is threefold. (1) The ceremonial or priestly law. (2) The civil or worldly law. (3) The law of the two tablets or the Ten Commandments. Each institution has its reason.

52. What is the purpose of the Levitical or Priestly Law?

God commanded the people of Israel to serve Him with sacrifices and other similar works of worship so that they might be a foreshadowing of Christ, just as He was to be sacrificed for us, *1 Corinthians 5*. Now that Christ has come in the flesh and has offered Himself for the sin of the world, the foreshadowing has ceased, *Colossians 2*, because with one offering, He has perfected forever those who are sanctified, *Hebrews 10*.

53. What is the benefit of the Civil or Judicial Law?

This was given by God to the Jewish people so that disputes could be resolved and evil men punished. It can also be useful in civil government for regulating public order, as it is employed in courts of law to maintain the well-being and state of the government, as far as it is necessary for the common good.

54. Does the Law of the Ten Commandments apply to us as well?

In every way, for God has not revoked it, and the Lord Christ has honored and explained it, *Matthew 5*. And it has great usefulness even among Christians in the world.

55. What is the benefit?

(1) It is useful to guide us to perfect service and love toward God, as stated in *Deuteronomy 6*: "You shall love the Lord your God with all your heart, with all your mind, and with all your strength, and your neighbor as yourself."

(2) It teaches us to live rightly before God, as it says in *Psalm 119*: "Your word is a lamp to my feet and a light to my path."

(3) When such governance is applied with proper occasion, it is beneficial. Therefore, the king in Israel should read the Book of the Law all his life, as written in *Deuteronomy 27*.

(4) It helps us recognize God's wrath against our sins, as stated in *Deuteronomy 27*: "Cursed is the one who does not confirm all the words of this law by observing them." And thus, the Law has become our tutor to bring us to Christ, as it says in *Galatians 3*.

56. Was not the Law given so that we might become saved through it?

No, for even though it says that the one who keeps these commandments will be saved (as written in *Leviticus 18*, "The person who follows My statutes shall live by them"), it is impossible to keep the commandments, and thus no one can be saved by them.

57. How do you recognize such an impossibility?

(1) St. Paul says in *Romans 3*: "It is entirely impossible for anyone to be justified and saved, for all people are under sin."

(2) Through the Law no one becomes righteous, alive, or saved, *Galatians 3*. It would only bring salvation if anyone could fulfill the Law.

13. Of the Gospel and God's Grace.

58. In such a way, must all people be condemned?

Indeed, unless God's mercy comes to their aid, as is proclaimed in the Gospel. *Lamentations 3*: "It is the Lord's mercies that we are not consumed." *Colossians 1*: "God has delivered us from the power of darkness."

59. What is the Gospel?

It is the joyful teaching of God's grace, that the merciful God has compassion on sinful people, gives them His Son as a Savior, reconciles them to God, and makes them heirs of His eternal Kingdom.

60. Does God's mercy extend to all people?

Yes, without distinction. (1) God declares this in *Romans 11*: "God has consigned all to disobedience, that He might have mercy on all." *2 Peter 3*: "God does not wish that anyone should perish, but that everyone should come to repentance." *1 Timothy 2*: "God wants all people should be saved and come to the knowledge of the truth." (2) God has sent His Son to all people as the Savior, *John 3*: "For God so loved the world, that He gave His only begotten Son." (3) God calls all people to salvation, *Matthew 11*: "Come unto Me, all ye that labor and are heavy laden, and I will give you rest."

61. If God seriously means this, must all people be saved?

God wills this grace for all, but it is the case that all must also come to the knowledge of the truth, *1 Timothy 2*; repent, *Ezekiel 18*; believe, and be baptized, *Mark 16*. Though all could be saved, it does not happen because most do not come to the knowledge of the truth, do not repent, do not believe, nor are baptized.

14. Of the Election of Grace.

62. Has God not chosen only certain people for His grace and salvation, and rejected the others for damnation?

No, instead all who come to the knowledge of the truth and persist in faith in Christ until death, He has chosen for salvation, those whom He has foreseen from eternity, that they will remain in faith in Christ, *Ephesians 1*. God has chosen us through Christ before the foundation of the world.

63. Is this election determined by God's counsel, or by man's merit?

It is not determined by a person's merit, but solely by God's mercy, *1 Timothy 1*: "God has saved us, not by our works, but according to His purpose and grace, which was given to us in Christ Jesus before the beginning of time." *Romans 11*: "If it is by grace, then it is no longer by works, otherwise grace would no longer be grace."

64. Nevertheless, has God chosen some and rejected others because it pleased Him to do so?

No. Rather, He has looked only to those who would receive the Lord Christ by faith, and thus has ordained believers to salvation, but has rejected the unbelievers, *John 3*: "Whoever believes in the Son is not judged; but whoever does not believe is already judged."

15. Of the Person of Christ.

65. Since our salvation rests entirely and solely on Christ, tell me, what must a Christian believe and hold concerning Christ?

Two things must be understood about Him: His Person and His Office.

66. Who is the Lord Christ in His Person?

He is true God and true Man, and yet only one Person. That He is God has already been proven. He is also true Man is shown in *Hebrews 2*: "Since the children have flesh and blood, He likewise became flesh and blood."

67. How? Have the divine and human natures become only one Person?

Just as body and soul are one person, so God and Man are one Christ, *John 1*: "The Word became flesh and dwelt among us." *Luke 1*: "The holy one born of you will be called the Son of God."

68. Have these natures shared their properties with one another?

Just as the soul imparts life and natural abilities such as seeing, hearing, etc., to the body, so the divine nature has imparted omnipotence and extraordinary efficacy to the human nature.

69. How do you prove that Christ is omnipotent according to His human nature?

Matthew 28: "All authority in heaven and on earth has been given to Me." *John 5*: "The Father has given the Son the power to execute judgment because He is the Son of Man."

70. Is it also stated in Scripture that Christ, as a man, is all-knowing?

Yes, indeed. *Colossians 2*: "In Christ are hidden all the treasures of wisdom and knowledge." In *John 2*, it is testified: "He knew all things." He also bears witness that He knew what was in a man.

71. Where is the omnipresence of Christ's humanity?

Ephesians 4: "Christ has ascended above all the heavens, that He might fill all things." *Matthew 18*: "Where two or three are gathered in My name, there I am among them." *Matthew 28*: "I am with you always, to the end of the age."

16. Of Christ's Humiliation.

72. Has Christ always exercised this glory as a man, or how did He walk in the form of a servant?

Christ, in His state of humiliation, laid aside His glory and appeared as a poor, degraded man so that He could fulfill His office by suffering and dying. But in His state of exaltation, He has used this glory.

73. What is the state of Christ's humiliation?

It is when Christ was conceived by His mother, born, raised, carried out His preaching office, then suffered, took on human weaknesses, and thus became like other men. As it is said, *Philippians 2*, "just as Jesus Christ was in the form of God, He did not consider equality with God something to be grasped, but He humbled Himself and became obedient unto death, even death on the cross."

17. Of Christ's Exaltation.

74. What does the state of His exaltation consist of?

It consists of His victorious descent into hell, resurrection from the dead, ascension into heaven, sitting at the right hand of God, and His return for the final judgment of the living and the dead.

75. What is Christ's descent into Hell?

It is a triumph in which Christ revealed Himself to the devil and hell as a conqueror. *Hosea 13:* "O death, I will be your poison! O hell, I will be your pestilence!" *Colossians 2:* "Christ disarmed the rulers and authorities, and made a public display of them, triumphing over them by Himself."

76. How did He rise again?

That on the third day He broke through death and gave life back to Himself, thus taking the full power over life and death into Himself.

77. How did Christ ascend into heaven?

He visibly ascended before the eyes of the apostles, and a cloud took Him from their sight, *Acts 1*. However, He ascended beyond all visible and created heavens, *Ephesians 4*, and entered into the heaven of divine majesty and glory, which is hidden from us humans. For when we say to God, "Our Father, who art in heaven," we understand by this the heaven of majesty and hidden light, *1 Timothy 6*. Thus, Christ is in heaven, meaning He has entered into His glory, *Luke 24*.

78. So, will Christ no longer be on earth when He has ascended to heaven?

Just as God is in heaven and yet fills both heaven and earth, *Jeremiah 23*, so Christ is in heaven and still subdues His enemies with power, *Psalm 110*. Therefore, He appeared bodily to Stephen, *Acts 7*, to Paul near Damascus, *Acts 9*, and in the barracks in Jerusalem, *Acts 23*. For He said, "Heaven and earth will all be filled," *Ephesians 4*.

79. What is meant by sitting at the right hand of God?

God's right hand signifies His almighty power, as it is written, *Psalm 77*. Thus it is said, Christ sits at the right hand of the power of God, *Luke 22*. This refers to the throne of majesty, *Hebrews 8*. Thus, Christ reigns. *Psalm 47*: "God is King over all nations. God sits on His holy throne." Therefore, sitting at the right hand of God signifies His eternal and mighty reign in divine majesty and glory. Thus, what is written in *Psalm 110*, "Sit at my right hand," is called by St. Paul "reigning," *1 Cor. 15*. (We will speak further about the Last Judgment later.)

18. Of Christ's Office.

80. What does Christ's Office consist of?

The office of the Lord Christ is threefold: (1) The Priestly, (2) the Prophetic, and (3) the Kingly.

81. What is the Priestly Office?

That Christ, through His obedience, the fulfillment of the Law, His suffering, and death, atoned for all sins of all people and redeemed us from God's judgment. *Galatians 4*: "When the fullness of time had come, God sent His Son, born of a woman, born under the law, to redeem those who were under the law, that we might receive adoption as sons."

82. Has Christ thus paid for the sins of mankind and taken their punishment upon Himself?

Yes: *Isaiah 53*: "Surely He took up our infirmities and carried our sorrows; He was pierced for our transgressions and crushed for our iniquities. The punishment that brought us peace was upon Him, and by His wounds we are healed." He is the atonement for our sins. *John 1*: "He is our propitiation through faith in His blood"; *Romans 3*: "Our redemption through His blood."

83. Has this payment been made for all people, or only for some?

For all people. *Genesis 12*: "In your seed, all the families of the earth will be blessed." *Isaiah 53*: "The Lord laid on Him the iniquity of us all." *2 Corinthians 5*: Christ died for all.

84. Has Christ paid for all the guilt of mankind, or must each person also atone for their own sin?

For all sins. *Isaiah 53:* "You have cast all my sins behind your back." *1 John 1:* "The blood of Jesus Christ, the Son of God, cleanses us from all sin." *Titus 2:* Christ gave Himself for us to redeem us from all iniquity.

85. Has Christ reconciled all people, how then is it that not all are saved?

The reason is that not all people make themselves receptive to this reconciliation, nor do they allow themselves to be led by God's saving works of grace to the grace He has acquired for them.

19. Of Christ's Prophetic Office.

86. What are these works of grace?

The works that belong to Christ's prophetic office are:
(1) The call to God's Word.
(2) Repentance.
(3) Conversion.
(4) Regeneration.
(5) Renewal.
(6) The laying aside of sins.
(7) Union with Christ.

20. Of God's Call to His Kingdom.

87. What is the calling that you speak of?

It is a gracious teaching about the calling: How poor sinful people are called to repentance, to the forgiveness of sins, and to conversion to an eternal kingdom of God, and how we are included in it.

88. Does God call all people in this way, or only some?

All, without distinction. For Christ Himself calls, *Matthew 11:* "Come to Me, all who labor and are heavy laden, and I will give you rest." He commanded the apostles, *Mark 16:* "Preach the Gospel to every creature." They faithfully carried this out. *Acts 17:* "God commands all people everywhere to repent."

89. Does this calling lead us to the eternal Kingdom of God?

Yes. For we are called to repentance and the forgiveness of sins, *Luke 24*, to the refreshment of the soul, *Matthew 11*, that we may come to completeness in Christ, *Colossians 1*, and be gathered under the wings of God's grace, *Matthew 23*.

21. Of Repentance.

90. What do you promised through repentance?

A recognition and earnest remorse for the sins committed, along with a firm confidence in God, that He will graciously forgive them on account of the holy merit of Christ.

91. Is it not enough that I sincerely repent of my sins?

No, for where there is true repentance, there is certainly also a serious remorse for sins, as Peter repented of his sin, *Matthew 26*, and the tax collector did not dare to lift his eyes to God, *Luke 18*, however, both Cain, *Genesis 4*, and Judas, *Matthew 27*, deeply regretted their sins, but still did not truly repent (because there was no faith nor steadfast confidence in God. Thus, in repentance, there must also be confidence in grace, as the Lord Christ said to the repentant sinner: "Your faith has saved you," *Luke 7*.

92. How can a person come to true repentance?

Not by their own strength; rather, God leads them to the recognition of sin through the Law. *Romans 3:* Through the Law comes the knowledge of sin. But confidence in divine grace is perceived through the Gospel, which continuously declares the forgiveness of sins through Christ, so that whoever believes in Him is justified, *Acts 13*.

93. What fruits come from repentance?

Twofold:

(1) That God does not despise such troubled and contrite hearts, *Psalm 51*, but rather chooses to dwell with them, *Isaiah 57*.

(2) That they guard themselves against sin, crucify their flesh, and resist their lusts and desires, *Galatians 5*.

22. On the Conversion to God.

94. What is conversion?

It is a turning away from unbelief, disobedience, and all sin, and from enmity against God and man. In contrast, it is a turning towards faith, obedience, and love toward God and one's neighbor. *Romans 13* says: "Let us cast off the works of darkness and put on the armor of light."

95. Can a person convert themselves, or promote their own conversion?

A person can certainly hear God's Word, just as Herod gladly heard John the Baptist, *Mark 6*. But he cannot turn his heart and mind on his own. For if we cannot make a single hair on our head white or black, *Matthew 5*, and can do nothing good without Christ, *John 15*, nor even think anything good—since no one can call God the Lord in their heart without the Holy Spirit, *1 Corinthians 12*, and cannot devise any good, *2 Corinthians 3*—so likewise, we cannot turn our hearts to God nor promote our own conversion toward good thoughts.

96. If God alone converts people, why does He not convert everyone?

It is God who works in us, both to will and to act according to His good pleasure, *Philippians 2*, and God certainly desires to help. But just as a wounded person cannot be healed if they reject the medicine and do not fully submit themselves to the doctor, likewise a person cannot be converted if they do not fully yield themselves to God's work. If they pursue worldly desires and worries, *Matthew 13*, resist the Holy Spirit, *Acts 7*, and do not bring their reasoning into obedience to Christ, *2 Corinthians 10*, they hinder God from accomplishing His work in them.

97. What, then, should a person do for their conversion?

They must hear God's Word, for faith comes from hearing it, *Romans 10*. They should not resist it in their flesh, *Acts 7*, but bring their reasoning into obedience to faith, *2 Corinthians 10*.

23. Of Justification before God.

98. Since all people are sinners and unrighteous, how are they made righteous before God?

No one is made righteous by their own merit or good works:

(1) (1.) All have sinned and fall short of the glory that we have in God, *Rom. 3*. *Deuteronomy 27*: "Cursed is the one who does not uphold all the words of this law by carrying them out."

(2) We owe all good works to God, and therefore they earn nothing. *Luke 17*: "When you have done everything you were commanded, say, 'We are unworthy servants; we have only done our duty.'"

(3) Furthermore, even if someone is mindful of doing good works, they earn nothing for God. *Matthew 15*: "In vain do they worship Me, teaching as doctrines the commandments of men."

99. Where does our righteousness come from?

It comes solely from Christ, who has been made our righteousness by God, *1 Corinthians 1*. We are saved from God's wrath through Him, after being made righteous through His blood, *Romans 4*. Therefore, it is said, "The Lord is our righteousness," *Jeremiah 23*.

100. How does a sinner become partaker of Christ's righteousness?

In this way: When I accept, with faithful trust, the fulfillment of the Law and the payment of the debt made by Christ for me, it no differently than if I had fully satisfied God for my sins myself.

24. Of Faith.

101. Explain to me how Christ's merit is reckoned to you through faith.

If someone pays a debt for another person and the debtor believes that the payment was made on his behalf, and he accepts it with gratitude, it is credited to him as if he had paid it himself. In the same way, when Christ presents Himself as having fully satisfied the divine judgment for all sins, I, as a sinner, accept this, rejoice before God, thank Him, and consider myself free. Thus, Christ's merit is credited to me in the same way, as if I had personally paid my debt to divine justice.

102. What, then, is justifying faith?

It is a certain confidence, where a person firmly believes in God the Lord, that all His marks of grace and promises of grace will absolve him, and therefore he has a gracious God toward him and possesses righteousness. *Hebrews 11*: "Faith is the certainty of what is hoped for and the conviction of what is not seen."

103. Does Holy Scripture attribute justification to faith?

Yes. *Acts 10*: "To this Jesus all the prophets bear witness, that through His name everyone who believes in Him receives forgiveness of sins." *Romans 3*: "We are justified freely by His grace through the redemption that is in Christ Jesus, whom God put forward as a propitiation by His blood, to be received by faith, so that He might demonstrate the righteousness that is valid before Him, in that He forgives sin."

104. Is the imputation of Christ's merit also founded in Holy Scripture?

Yes. *Genesis 15:6*: "Abraham believed the Lord, and He counted it to him as righteousness." *Romans 4:5*: "To the one who does not work but believes in Him who justifies the ungodly, his faith is counted as righteousness." *Isaiah 53:6*: "The Lord has laid on Him the iniquity of us all." Thus, we are made righteous when Christ's righteousness is imputed to us. *2 Corinthians 5:21*: "God made Him who knew no sin to be sin for us, that in Him we might become the righteousness of God."

105. Do we have examples of holy people who imputed Christ's merit to themselves by faith?

Yes, St. Paul speaks of himself in *Galatians 2:20*: "The Son of God loved me and gave Himself for me." And the Virgin Mary said in *Luke 1:46–47*: "My soul magnifies the Lord, and my spirit rejoices in God my Savior."

25. Of Regeneration.

106. What does regeneration consist of?

In two parts. First, that one gives up the evil life and does not follow the evil natural lusts, but rather resists them to the utmost; this is called putting to death the old man, *Romans 6*, and crucifying the flesh along with its lusts and desires, *Galatians 5:24*.

107. What is the second part of regeneration?

That all human faculties are awakened to a God-pleasing life: the *understanding* recognizes spiritual things, *1 Corinthians 2:14*, the *will* lives in true righteousness and holiness, *Ephesians 4:24*, and we *walk* in a new life, *Romans 6:4*.

108. Is a person not changed in his substance and nature by regeneration?

No. (1) For no man is completely pure. *Pro. 20:9*: "Who can say: I have made my heart clean; I am pure from my sin?" (2) There always remains the struggle between the flesh and the spirit in every regenerate person. *Gal. 5:17*: "The flesh desires against the spirit, and the spirit against the flesh." (3) And even the reborn must confess, *Psa. 51*, "I am conceived in sin." (4) The reborn must die and return to the earth, *Gen. 3:19*: "For this reason they still have sinful flesh in them."

26. Of Renewal.

109. What is renewal?

It is nothing other than the common putting off of the sinful life by the reborn and the adopting of a new life that is pleasing to God.

110. What does the Holy Scripture say about these works?

Ephesians 4 says: "Put off, in regard to your former conduct, the old man, which is corrupt according to deceitful lusts; and be renewed in the spirit of your mind, and put on the new man, which is created according to God in true righteousness and holiness."

27. Of the Union with Christ.

111. Are the reborn people united with Christ?

Yes. *Ephesians 5:* "Do you not know that your bodies are members of Christ?" He who joins with the Lord is one spirit with Him.

112. Does this union happen through an essential transformation into Christ's flesh?

No. How could such bodies otherwise be mortal if they were essentially Christ's body? How could the body breathe, or how could it be glorified and spiritual on the last day? But the union that happens here, and happens through faith, is that a person joins with God through trust and completely commits themselves to Him.

113. Does God perform all these works of grace through or without means?

Through three means: (1) Through the Holy Scripture, (2) through the holy Sacraments, and (3) through the preaching office.

28. Of the Holy Scripture.

114. How does it happen through the Holy Scripture?

When we hear or read it. The Lord Christ admonishes, *John 5,* "Search the Scriptures, for they are the ones that testify of Me." Salvation-bringing faith comes from the Scripture, *Romans 10,* "Faith comes from hearing, and hearing through the Word of God," and salvation comes through faith, *2 Timothy 3:15,* "From childhood, you have known the Holy Scriptures, which are able to make you wise for salvation through faith in Christ Jesus." Therefore, the Scripture is a power of God for salvation to those who believe, *Romans 1.*

29. Of the Holy Sacraments.

115. What do you understand by the Sacraments?

They are holy divinely-ordained acts, in which God gives us something heavenly along with the earthly, so that through them God's promises of grace are confirmed, sealed, and applied, and we are made partakers of God's spiritual gifts.

116. Explain to me a bit more how the Sacraments are seals?

When God declares in His Word that He wills all people to be saved, each believer concludes: "God wills that I, too, shall be saved. This is further confirmed for me when God, in my Baptism, makes a covenant with me and promises me that I shall be His beloved child. Likewise, when Christian faith tells me that Christ, who died for all, has redeemed me, I grasp hold of this assurance with Christ in the Lord's Supper: 'Take, eat, this is My body, given for you for the forgiveness of your sins. Drink, this is My blood, shed for you for the forgiveness of your sins.' Thus, the Sacraments confirm my faith, so that I take God's promise as my own."

117. Can you make it clearer with a comparison?

Just as God promised all people, "There will no longer be a flood to cover the earth," and confirmed His word with the rainbow as a seal and visible sign, *Genesis 9:13*, and when He promised King Hezekiah health, He gave him a sign of assurance by making the shadow on the sundial go backward. In the same way, what God has promised regarding salvation, He confirms through the Sacraments, as through seals and visible signs.

118. How many Sacraments are there?

Two: Holy Baptism and the Lord's Supper.

30. Of Holy Baptism.

119. What is Baptism?

It is a spiritual action ordained by Christ, in which a person is either immersed in or sprinkled with water in the name of God the Father, the Son, and the Holy Spirit. Through Baptism, the person becomes a partaker of Christ's merit, receives forgiveness of sins, is taken into God's covenant, and is accepted as a child of God and an heir to eternal salvation.

120. Must all people be baptized?

Yes, according to Christ's command: "Teach all nations and baptize them," *Matthew 28*. And in His teaching and warning, *John 3*: "Unless one is born of water and the Spirit, he cannot enter the kingdom of God."

121. Should little children also be baptized?

Yes, because (1) children belong to the kingdom of God, *Mark 10*, but no one can enter the kingdom of heaven without baptism, *John 3*. And (2) in the Old Testament, children were circumcised when they were only eight days old, *Genesis 17*, so holy Baptism should not be denied to children.

122. Can any Christian perform Baptism?

Baptism should ideally be administered by the preaching office, as Christ said to the apostles, *Matthew 28*: "Teach all nations and baptize them." However, if a preacher cannot be found quickly, another person may baptize in an emergency. For (1) all believing Christians are one in Christ, *Galatians 3*; (2) in emergencies, wise individuals may teach, *Romans 16*; therefore, they may also baptize. (3) Similarly, Moses' wife circumcised her sons, *Exodus 4*, and the Jewish women also performed this, as shown in *Maccabees*.

123. What benefit does Baptism bring?

(1) It gives a person the renewal of the Holy Spirit, *Titus 3*.
(2) It brings the forgiveness of sins, *Acts 2*.
(3) It establishes a covenant with God, *1 Peter 3*.
(4) And it grants eternal life. *1 Peter 3*: Baptism makes us saved.

31. Of the Lord's Supper.

124. What is the Lord's Supper?

It is a spiritual action ordained by Christ, in which Christians receive under the blessed bread His body to eat, and under the blessed wine His blood to drink, so that through it His promises in the Gospel are fulfilled, shown to each one, sealed, the faith is strengthened, and they are thus fed and nourished unto eternal life.

125. What actually belongs to this Sacrament?

Two things: an earthly one, bread and wine; and a heavenly one, the body and blood of the Lord Christ.

126. How do you prove that Christ's body and blood are eaten and drunk in the Holy Supper?

First, because Christ explicitly says: "This is My body. Drink, this is My blood." Then, because the bread and the cup of the Lord's Supper are called the *communion* or *participation* in the body and blood of Christ, *1 Corinthians 10:16.*

127. Is it not enough that one remembers Christ's merit during the reception of bread and wine and thereby receives His body and blood spiritually through faith?

No, for the eating and drinking which occurs with faith[4] were also established in the Old Testament. It [spiritual eating] can, outside of the Sacrament, be rightly performed at any time without bread and wine and still be beneficial, since no one believes in Christ to their condemnation. However, the eating and drinking that takes place in the Holy Supper belongs solely to the New Testament. It cannot be done without bread and wine, nor rightly performed outside of the Sacrament. It can also be received to one's condemnation, as stated in *1 Corinthians 11:27–29:* "Whoever eats this bread or drinks the cup of the Lord in an unworthy manner will be guilty of sinning against the body and blood of the Lord. For anyone who eats

---

4 He is making the distinction here between spiritual and sacramental eating.

and drinks without recognizing the body of the Lord eats and drinks judgment on themselves."

128. What benefit is there in the use of the Holy Supper?

Firstly, my faith is strengthened by it. For when I believe from God's Word that Christ has loved me and given Himself for me, since He is the Lamb of God who bears the sin of the world, then the Lord Christ comes in the Holy Supper, gives me His body to eat and His blood to drink, and says: "Take, eat, this is My body and blood given and shed for you for the forgiveness of sins." Thus, He strengthens the very faith that I have drawn from the Word of grace.

Secondly, I am given a pledge of life and salvation. For since I have partaken of the body and blood of the One who lives forever and has brought me life, I too shall partake in life, as it is said in *John 14.*

32. Of the Holy Ministry.

129. What do you call the Office of Preaching?

It is an office ordained by God, in which He has appointed certain persons from among men, that they, with divine authority and standing, as ambassadors in His place, proclaim the Word of their Lord, distribute the Sacraments according to His institution, and thus lead people to Christ and raise them to eternal life.

130. What word are preachers to proclaim to their congregation?

Only the Word of God, as it says in *Matthew 28,* "Teach them to observe all that I have commanded you." This is what the prophets and apostles have left us in writing, from which Christian faith comes, *Romans 10,* and is the power of God unto salvation for those who believe, *Romans 1.* The whole sum of this consists of the Law and the Gospel, which have already been discussed.

131. Do preachers, besides the Word, have other means by which they lead people to God?

Alongside the Word, they must also lead people with good

example, *1 Timothy 4*: "Be an example to the believers, in word, in conduct, in love, in spirit, in faith, in purity." And they must also use the authority of the keys, as Christ says, *John 20*: "Whosoever sins you remit, they are remitted unto them, and whosoever sins you retain, they are retained." *Matthew 18*: "Whatever you bind on earth shall also be bound in heaven, and whatever you loose on earth shall also be loosed in heaven."

132. How is a person led to God through the key of absolution?

This happens when the preacher, with divine authority, forgives the person's sins, and that person, with great love and trust, approaches God and calls upon Him as "dear Father," *Romans 8*, because they are certain that they are in grace with God, as a child is with their father.

133. How does one come to God through the key of binding?

When a stubborn sinner is warned of God's wrath and is frightened so that they recognize their sins and seek forgiveness from God, as St. Paul wrote about the sinner at Corinth: "I have decided to deliver such a one to Satan for the destruction of the flesh, so that the spirit may be saved in the day of the Lord Jesus," *1 Corinthians 5*.

134. So, is salvation a fruit of the Preaching Office?

Yes. The Lord Christ commanded St. Paul and confirms it as follows: "I send you to the Gentiles to open their eyes, so that they may turn from darkness to light and from the power of Satan to God, to receive forgiveness of sins and an inheritance among those who are sanctified by faith in Me," *Acts 26:18*. And again, St. Paul writes: "Devote yourself to the public reading of Scripture, to exhortation, to teaching; for if you do this, you will save both yourself and those who hear you," *1 Timothy 4:13, 16*. And in order for this to happen, the preaching office gathers people into the Christian Church, so that it may lead them to Christ, as a bride to her bridegroom, *2 Corinthians 11:2*.

33. Of the Christian Church.

135. What is the Christian Church?

It is a gathering of those who confess themselves to be part of Christ's Kingdom, where God's Word is taught purely and the Sacraments are administered according to Christ's institution and order.

136. Who belongs to the Christian Church?

God indeed wills that all people should come into it, *Acts 10:35*: "In every nation, anyone who fears Him and does what is right is acceptable to Him." And although, outwardly, all those who hear God's Word and make use of the Sacraments according to Christ's command are within it, yet only true believers are the rightful members of the Christian Church, *Ephesians 3:17*: "Christ dwells in your hearts through faith."

137. What are the characteristics of the Christian Church?

There are primarily four: (1) Innocence, (2) Unity, (3) Perseverance, and, (4) Blameless Truth.

138. What is the Church's innocence?

That Christ has cleansed her from all sins through His blood, *John 17*. Also, through the washing of water with the Word, He has sanctified and purified her, making her glorious, without spot or wrinkle or anything of the sort, but that she may be holy and blameless, *Ephesians 5:25–26*.

139. What do you understand by unity?

That all believers are united with Christ through faith, *Ephesians 5*, and also with each other as one body, *1 Corinthians 12*. Of this, the Apostle writes: "One body and one Spirit, just as you were called to one hope of your calling: One Lord, one faith, one baptism, one God and Father of all," *Ephesians 4*.

140. How is the Christian Church enduring?

That it cannot be overcome by the gates of hell, *Matthew 16,* but that there will always remain a remnant of devout Christians on earth, according to Daniel's prophecy, chapter 4: "A kingdom will be established from heaven that shall never be destroyed."

141. How does the Church possess infallible truth?

Through the fact that there will never be a lack of people in the world who have the true, saving faith. Hence, the Christian Church is called "a pillar and ground of the truth," *2 Timothy 3.*

142. How is the Christian Church recognized?

It has two main distinguishing marks:

(1) The pure preaching of the Gospel.

(2) The right use of the holy Sacraments according to Christ's institution.

143. How do you prove this concerning the preaching of the Gospel?

John 10:27, the Lord Christ says: "My sheep hear My voice." And *John 14:23:* "Whoever loves Me will keep My word."

144. Do we also read the same concerning the Sacraments?

1 Corinthians 12:12–13: "For we were all baptized by one Spirit into one body, and we were all given one Spirit to drink."

145. Does the Christian Church have the authority to arrange matters of religion as it pleases?

In the Divine Service [*Gottesdienst*] itself, it can and should not ordain anything. However, concerning the ceremonies [*Ceremonien*] used in worship, the Church may arrange as it wishes, provided that it considers:

(1) God's glory. *1 Corinthians 10:31:* "Whatever you do, do it all for the glory of God."

(2) The edification of others. *1 Corinthians 14:26:* "Let all things be done for edification."

(3) Good order and consistency. *1 Corinthians 14:40:* "Let all things be done decently and in order."

(4) Christian freedom. *Galatians 5:1:* "Stand firm in the freedom by which Christ has made us free."

146. Is the Christian Church divided into certain estates?

Yes, into three estates:

(1) The first is the estate of teaching, which has already been discussed.

(2) The second is the governing estate, *Romans 13:1:* "Let every person be subject to the governing authorities; for there is no authority except from God."

(3) The household estate, in which parents and children, masters and servants, live according to the fourth commandment.

34. Of the state of people after death.

147. What is the state of believers when they die?

Believers are like unbelievers in: (1) Death, (2) The resurrection, (3) And the Last Judgment; but they are entirely different in the state of salvation and condemnation.

148. What is death?

It is the separation of the body and the soul, where the body returns to the earth, but the soul is brought either into eternal salvation or eternal damnation, as is known from the story of the rich man and Lazarus, *Luke 16.*

149. Where do human souls go after death?

The souls of the righteous are in God's hand, where no torment touches them, *Wisdom 3:1.* They are carried by angels to Abraham's bosom, where they are comforted, *Luke 16:22–25.* But the souls of the unbelievers go to the place of torment, *Luke 16:28,* to the darkness where there will be weeping and gnashing of teeth, *Matthew 22:13,* to the pit that burns with sulfur and pitch, *Revelation 21:8,* and to the eternal fire prepared for the devil and his angels, *Matthew 25:41.*

150. Do the souls of believers go to purgatory to be cleansed of their remaining sins?

No. (1) Because Holy Scripture teaches nothing about it. (2) Because believers immediately enter into rest at death, *Revelation 14:13:* "Blessed are the dead who die in the Lord from now on; yes, says the Spirit, that they may rest from their labors." (3) And the thief who was crucified with Christ reached salvation without such a purging, *Luke 23:43:* "Today you will be with me in Paradise."

151. Will all people rise from the dead?

Yes: *John 5:28:* "The hour is coming in which all who are in the graves will hear the voice of the Son of Man and will come forth: those who have done good, to the resurrection of life, and those who have done evil, to the resurrection of judgment."

152. Will the believers not have a better body in the resurrection than they had in this world?

The very same body that died will rise again, *Job 19:26:* "I will be clothed with this, my own skin, and in my flesh, I will see God." But it will have a better condition than it had with that same body.

153. What is this condition?

In general, St. Paul describes it this way: "It is sown perishable, and it is raised imperishable; it is sown in dishonor, and it is raised in glory; it is sown in weakness, and it is raised in power. It is sown a natural body, and it is raised a spiritual body," *1 Corinthians 15:42–44.*

154. What special gifts does a spiritual body have?

Chiefly these:

(1) Heavenly brightness. *Mat. 13:43:* "The righteous will shine like the sun in their Father's kingdom."

(2) Invisibility. The Lord Christ vanished from His disciples, *Luke 24:31,* and those who rise with Him will be seen by those to whom they appear, *Mat. 13:43.*

(3) Immortality. *1 Cor. 15:53:* The perishable must clothe itself with the imperishable, and the mortal with immortality.

(4) Complete bodily strength, *Mat. 13:43*.

(5) Perfect bodily beauty. *1 Cor. 15:49*: "Just as we have borne the image of the earthly man, so shall we bear the image of the heavenly man."

(6) Eternal enjoyment of glorious joy and righteousness. *Rev. 7:16*: "They will hunger no more, nor thirst anymore, neither will the sun strike them, nor any scorching heat."

36. Of the Last Day.

155. Will Christ not establish a glorious kingdom on earth before the Last Day?

No. (1) The last times of the world will be dreadful times, *2 Tim. 3:1*, so that when the Son of Man comes for judgment, He will scarcely find faith on earth, *Luke 18:8*.

(2) The dead, who belong to Christ's kingdom, will not rise before the Last Day. *John 6:40*: "I will raise him up on the Last Day." And concerning Lazarus, his sister says, *John 11:24*: "I know well that he will rise again in the resurrection on the Last Day."

37. Of the Last Judgment.

156. Will a universal judgment come upon mankind on the Last Day?

Yes. *Matthew 25:31–32*: "Before Him, the Judge, all nations will be gathered." *2 Corinthians 5:10*: "We must all appear before the judgment seat of Christ."

157. Will this judgment take place at the end of the world?

Yes. *Matthew 13:40–43*: "Just as the weeds are gathered and burned with fire, so it will be at the end of this world. The Son of Man will send His angels, and they will gather out of His kingdom all causes of sin and all evildoers, and throw them into the fiery furnace; there will be weeping and gnashing of teeth. Then the righteous will shine like the sun in the kingdom of their Father."

158. Will the world completely perish and come to nothing at that time?

Yes. *Luke 21:33*, Christ says: "Heaven and earth will pass away." *Psalm 102:26–27*: "The heavens are the work of your hands; they will perish, but you will endure."

159. What matters will be dealt with before the Last Judgment?

Everything that people have ever done will be brought forth. *Ecclesiastes 12:14*: "God will bring every deed into judgment, including everything hidden." *Matthew 12:36*: "People will give account on the day of judgment for every careless word they have spoken." *1 Corinthians 4:5*: "The Lord will bring to light what is hidden in darkness and will expose the motives of the heart."

160. What will the judgment say?

The judgment will be spoken to the righteous: "Come, you blessed of My Father, inherit the kingdom prepared for you from the foundation of the world." But to the unrighteous: "Depart from Me, you cursed, into the eternal fire prepared for the devil and his angels."

38. Of Eternal Blessedness.

161. What is the kingdom that is prepared for the righteous?

It is the kingdom of glory, in which there will be no more sorrow. *Revelation 21:4*: "Death will be no more, neither will there be mourning, nor crying, nor pain anymore, but joy and bliss will overtake them, and sighing and longing will be done away with." *1 Corinthians 2:9*: "No eye has seen, no ear has heard, nor has it entered into the heart of man, what God has prepared for those who love Him."

39. Of Eternal Damnation.

162. What is this eternal fire into which the damned will be cast?

It is eternal damnation, in which there will be no joy, nor blessedness, not even a drop of water or any comfort to be attained in hellish torment, *Luke 16:24*. On the contrary, the pain will be unimaginable and without end. *2 Thessalonians 1:9:* "They will suffer eternal destruction away from the presence of the Lord and from the glory of His might." *Revelation 20:10:* "They will be tormented day and night, forever and ever." *Mark 9:44:* "Their worm will not die, and their fire will not be quenched."

Lord God, merciful and gracious, patient and abounding in steadfast love and faithfulness; grant me, according to Your glorious mercy, Your great love, with which You have loved me, a person dead in sins, even before the foundation of the world was laid, and appointed me to sonship and eternal inheritance in heaven, to recognize this with thankfulness, and that I firmly trust in Your true Word of grace and also its seals, the Holy Sacraments. May I firmly rely on the promised fatherly grace, seeking my righteousness and salvation solely in Christ Jesus and His precious merit in firm faith in this, my only Helper and Throne of Grace, persevering until the end, and thus depart in blessedness, rise joyfully, and in His eternal Kingdom be comforted with unspeakable and glorious joy, without ceasing, for the sake of my highly deserving Savior's bitter suffering, death, victorious resurrection, and powerful intercession. Amen.

The Second Part.—On the Godly Life.

1. On the Godly Life.

1. What constitutes a godly life?
In that I refrain from all that is evil and sinful and I strive for all that is good and godly.

2. What do you mean by "evil and sinful," and conversely, "good and godly"?
Everything that God has commanded is good and godly; everything that He has forbidden is evil and sinful.

3. Where do you find such commandments and prohibitions of God?
First in my conscience, which tells me that I should honor God, fear authority, kill or harm no one, live chastely, take nothing from anyone, and bear no false witness, etc. Then I find this also in the Ten Commandments.

4. How can you properly divide all this?
As Christ divides the whole Law into the love of God and the love of one's neighbor, *Matthew 22:37–39.*

2. Of God's Love.

5. Which commandments teach the love of God?
The first three commandments, which are commonly called the first table [of the Law].

6. What does the first commandment require?
Three things: That I should (1) fear God above all things, (2) love Him, and (3) trust in Him.

In Childlike Fear.

7. How can you love God when you are supposed to fear Him?

Just as a child loves his father because he shows him all good things, and therefore fears to anger him and lose his goodness. In the same way, I love God because He shows me fatherly goodness and I live carefully in fear that I do not anger Him with any sin, turn away His goodness from me, nor, through stubborn wickedness, cast away His eternal kingdom from myself. This is a childlike fear.

8. How must you live according to such fear of God?

In this way: that I constantly remember that God sees everything that people do, *Sirach 23:18*. I see it as a serious duty to live according to the commandments, prayers, words, and works because I will one day give an account for my actions, *Mat. 12:46*, and also for those things hidden in darkness, *1 Cor. 4:5*. Therefore, I must live in fear and trembling, that I do not desire things that would lead to death.

Love.

9. What does God's love require?

It requires that God, as the highest good, be loved above all things, and that everything else be considered of lesser value. *Psalm 73:25, 26*: "Lord, if I only have You! I ask for nothing in heaven or on earth; even if I lose body and soul, You are still my God, all my heart's comfort and my portion." *Philippians 3:8*: "I count everything as loss compared to the surpassing worth of knowing Christ Jesus, my Lord, for whose sake I have lost all things and consider them rubbish, that I may gain Christ." *Matthew 10:37*: "Whoever loves father or mother more than Me is not worthy of Me. And whoever loves son or daughter more than Me is not worthy of Me."

10. Why should you love God so highly?

Because He loves me. *1 John 4:19*: "We love because He first loved us." He shows His love for me in that Christ died for me. *Ro-*

mans 5:8: "God demonstrates His love for us in this: While we were still sinners, Christ died for us." He gave His Son for me and, with Him, graciously gives me all things. *Romans 8:32:* "He who did not spare His own Son, but gave Him up for us all—how will He not also, along with Him, graciously give us all things?" He has preserved me from my mother's womb and does all good for me. *Sirach 50:24:* And He desires to give me His eternal kingdom. How could I not love Him in return?

11. Does God's love not also allow that you love creatures?

God has commanded me to love my neighbor as myself, *Leviticus 19:18.* He also commands me to love my enemies, *Matthew 5:44.* God has not commanded me to hate any creature; rather, I must love all things as God's works and gifts. But I must love Him above all and more than my own life. *Luke 14:26.*

12. But doesn't Christ say that we should hate our parents, children, and even ourselves? *Luke 14:26.*

Christ has not commanded me to go against the fourth and fifth commandments, or against Christian love, by hating anyone, including myself. Rather, He teaches that I should consider all friends, and even myself, as lesser, as enemies, compared to Christ, whom I should hold higher and dearer. And I should follow His word: "Whoever loves father, mother, son, or daughter more than Me is not worthy of Me."

And Trust.

13. What is the trust referred to in the first commandment?

When I fear and love God sincerely, I must also trust Him, that He will sustain me, just as a father sustains his child, and that nothing evil will befall me. Therefore, all adversity, persecution, illness, etc., that I encounter is a fatherly chastisement. *Hebrews 12:5:* "My son, do not take lightly the discipline of the Lord, and do not lose heart when He rebukes you. For the Lord disciplines those He loves, and He chastens every son He accepts." *1 Peter 4:1:* "Whoever suffers in the flesh has ceased from sin." And so, all things must work together for the good of those who love God, *Romans 8:28.*

14. What else belongs to this?

That I (2) believe my God will fulfill what He has spoken to me. *Psalm 33:4:* "The word of the Lord is faithful, and what He promises, He will certainly fulfill." Thus, like Abraham, I must grow strong in faith, believing in hope, even when by nature and worldly appearances there is nothing to hope for, and I must know with absolute certainty that what God has promised, He will also do, *Romans 4:20–21.*

In Words.

15. What does the second commandment require?

That I confess outwardly with my mouth the love I bear to God in my heart. *Matthew 12:34:* "For out of the abundance of the heart, the mouth speaks."

16. How does this happen?

(1) That I allow no corrupt talk to proceed from my mouth, nor any shameful word, foolish speech, or jesting, which are unbecoming for Christians, *Ephesians 4:29, 5:4.* Nor should I let any idle word be heard from me, *Matthew 12:36,* much less dishonor God's holy name with sinful speech such as cursing, swearing, sorcery, lying, or deceit. For the Lord will not hold anyone guiltless who misuses His name, *Exodus 20:7.*

(2) That I keep God's name holy and glorious in my heart, and promote His honor among others, as David promises the Lord, *Psalm 51:15:* "I will teach transgressors your ways, and sinners shall turn to you."

(3) That I call upon God in all distress, *Psalm 50:15:* "Call upon Me in the day of trouble; I will deliver you, and you shall glorify Me," following David's example, *Psalm 18:7:* "When I am in distress, I call upon the Lord, and cry to my God."

(4) That I give God praise and thanks for all His works of

grace. *Psalm 103:2:* "Bless the Lord, O my soul, and forget not all His benefits." *Colossians 5:20:* "Give thanks always and for everything to God the Father in the name of our Lord Jesus Christ."

In outward worship.[5]

17. How is the Sabbath day sanctified according to the third commandment?

(1) That I refrain from all labor at all times, as God says in this commandment: "Six days you shall labor and do all your work, but the seventh day is a Sabbath to the Lord your God; on it you shall not do any work."

(2) That I observe the spiritual day of rest, refrain from all evil works, and make it my concern to continue this rest throughout my life.

(3) That I spend the holy day with sacred thoughts, words, and deeds, but especially attend to the public worship [*Gottesdienstes*] of God.

18. What does the Divine Service consist of?

It is carried out in four parts:

(1) In hearing and obeying God's Word, (2) in prayer, (3) in thanksgiving, and (4) in the proper use of the holy Sacraments.

1. In Hearing of God's Word.

19. What is the divine Word that one should hear?

It is that which is contained in the prophetic and apostolic writings. I should eagerly hear it, explain it, live by it, and apply it for my constant use. *Luke 16:29:* "They have Moses and the Prophets; let them hear them." *Matthew 28:20:* "Teach them to observe all things that I have commanded you."

20. Should you not hear the Word which God might speak to you directly without other means?

---

5 *In äußerlichen Gottesdienst.*

Such a Word has not been promised to me by God. The Lord Christ preached orally, *Matthew 4:17*, and He also commanded His disciples to do the same, *Mark 16:15*. And God no longer speaks to us directly as He did in the past to the fathers, *Hebrews 1:1*. Moreover, false lights—Satan can disguise himself as an angel of light and present his word to me as if it were God's Word—so I must not listen to such a word.

21. But isn't there greater power in the direct Word from God than in the spoken word?

The preached word is a divine power and divine wisdom, *1 Corinthians 1:24*, a power of God that brings salvation to all who believe in it, *Romans 1:16*. Through this, hearts are moved, *Acts 2:37*, so that the grace of Christ has been received in all the world, *Colossians 1:6*. However, true Christians know nothing about the power of an immediate, direct Word from God in this time.

22. Isn't it enough when you have heard God's Word?

No, I must hear it in such a way that I also do it and bear its fruit. The Lord Christ says, *Matthew 7:24*, "Whoever hears My words and does them is like a wise man who builds his house on a rock." *Luke 8:15*, "The seed that falls on good ground is for those who hear the word, keep it in a noble and good heart, and bear fruit with patience."

23. What is this fruit?

There are two kinds. First, that I trust in the promises of grace from the Gospel, place my confidence solely in God, and let nothing worldly separate me from His love, *Romans 8:39*, and hold fast to His precious pledge until that day, *2 Timothy 1:12*. The second is that I learn to live a holy life, as God is holy, *1 Peter 1:15*, let my light shine before men, *Matthew 5:16*, and lead a good life before everyone, *1 Peter 2:12*. In summary, that I believe as a Christian and live a holy life.

2. In Prayer.

24. Why should you offer your prayer in the congregation, when Christ commands us to pray alone in a private room? *Matthew 6:6.*

Christ wants us to avoid seeking praise from people through prayer, and rather to pray alone in a private room. However, in the congregation, I should join other Christians in prayer, for such communal prayer is pleasing to God and is all the more powerful. *Matthew 18:19:* "Again, I say to you, if two of you agree on earth about anything they ask, it will be done for them by My Father in heaven."

25. Is it true prayer if it is spoken or sung aloud?

True prayer must come from the heart or soul, otherwise, it is not a prayer, whether it is sung or spoken. *1 Corinthians 14:15* says: "I will pray with the spirit, and I will pray with the understanding also." Men should lift up holy hands without anger or doubt. But if the prayer is only words from the mouth, while the heart is full of anger, doubt, etc., then it is not a true prayer. *Isaiah 29:13:* "This people draws near with their mouth and honors Me with their lips, but their heart is far from Me." *Isaiah 1:15:* "Though you make many prayers, I will not listen, for your hands are full of blood." *Sirach 34:29:* "If one prays and then curses again, how can the Lord hear him?"

26. What benefit is there, then, in praying with the mouth?

Since the mouth speaks from the overflow of the heart, *Matthew 12:34,* vocal prayer is a testimony of the prayer and devotion within the heart, which also encourages others to pray devoutly. Therefore, when heart and mouth are in agreement, the prayer is true. *Lamentations 3:41:* "Let us lift up our hearts with our hands unto God in heaven."

27. How and what should you pray?

I can best understand all this from the Lord's Prayer.

(Whom.)[6]

28. Whom should you call upon in prayer?

God as my Father; namely, God the Father; *John 16:23*: "Truly, truly, I say to you, whatever you ask of the Father in My name, He will give it to you." Also, God the Son, who is called the Eternal Father, *Isaiah 9:6*, and God the Holy Spirit, God the Holy Spirit [who has] begotten me anew as my Father. *John 3:5–6*.

29. May one call upon the holy angels or deceased saints?

No:

(1) Because I have no divine command for it.

(2) No promise that I will be heard in such a way.

(3) No example to follow in this regard.

(4) And since the angels and I are fellow servants and not my fathers, they do not desire to be worshiped by me. *Revelation 19:10*.

(5) Instead, I should worship God and serve Him alone. *Matthew 4:10*.

(With what kind of affection.)

30. How must you rightly call upon God?

This is shown to me partly by the opening and partly by the conclusion of the Lord's Prayer.

31. What does the introduction teach about this?

Firstly, that I call upon God as my Father; then the word "My" is a true word of faith, as we read in the 18th *Psalm*, verses 2 and 3: "I love You dearly, Lord, my strength. Lord, my rock, my fortress, and my deliverer; my God, my refuge, in whom I trust, my shield, and the horn of my salvation, and my stronghold." And it is an indication that I should address God with complete trust. Therefore, I must confidently trust Him, that He is disposed towards me as a father towards his child; *Isaiah 49:15*: "Can a woman forget her nursing

---

6 Hunnius offers a series of further divisions of the topic of "Prayer" which are so designated with parentheses.

child, that she should not have compassion on the son of her womb? Even if she forgets, I will not forget you." *Matthew 7:9–11:* "Which one of you, if his son asks him for bread, will give him a stone? Or if he asks for a fish, will give him a serpent? If you then, who are evil, know how to give good gifts to your children, how much more will your Father in heaven give good things to those who ask Him?"

32. Is there something more to remember in the introduction?

Secondly, that I call upon God as *our* Father; then the word "Our" also commands me to pray for others as well as for myself; namely, for all people. *1 Timothy 2:1* says: "I urge, then, first of all, that petitions, prayers, intercession, and thanksgiving be made for all people."

33. Why do you say to God: "Who art in heaven"?

So that I do not regard Him as an earthly father, who cannot always help his children or might not always want to, or who denies them when they need him most. Rather, I see Him as a heavenly Father, who alone possesses immortality, *1 Timothy 6:16*, and whose hand is not too short to save, *Isaiah 59:1*.

34. How does the conclusion teach you to pray correctly?

It teaches two things: First, that I bring to mind before God the reason why He should hear me.

(1) Because the Kingdom is His, and His Son is obligated to help His subjects.

(2) Because the Kingdom is His and everything that can help us belongs to Him. When He speaks, it happens; when He commands, it stands. This was spoken by the centurion in Capernaum, *Matthew 8:8:* "Speak only a word, and my servant will be healed."

(3) Because the glory is His forever; that is, because He commands us in *Psalm 50:15:* "Call upon Me in the day of trouble; I will deliver you, and you shall glorify Me." This results in eternal praise and glory for Him, as I will thank Him for being so gracious, and His goodness endures forever, *Psalm 136:1*. And we call upon Him, *Revelation 4:8:* "Holy, holy, holy is the Lord God Almighty!"

35. What is the other [thing]?

That with the word "Amen," I should testify that I hold trust in God that He will hear me concerning that for which I have prayed, for "Amen" means as much as "Yes, yes, it shall be so," as David explains it in *2 Samuel 7:28*: "Now, O Lord, You are God, and Your words will be truth."

(What should be prayed for.)

36. What is your desire that you may present before God?

Twofold: (1) That God would bestow upon me necessary goods in the first four petitions[7]; (2) That God would protect me from all evil, in the last three petitions.

(A. Spiritual Goods.)

37. What kind of goods are these, for which you yourself pray?

Spiritual, in the first three petitions, and physical, in the fourth.

(Sanctification of the Divine Name.)

38. How is God's name sanctified, as requested in the first petition?

God's name is sanctified among us when I seek God's glory in all things: "For, as Your name, so is Your praise," *Psalm 48:10*.

(1) When I receive God's word as God's word, *1 Thessalonians 2:13*.

(2) When I do everything for God's glory, *1 Corinthians 10:31*.

(3) When I live a holy life, just as the Lord my God is holy, *1 Peter 1:15*.

(4) When I hold the Divine Service of God in high regard; *Psalm 27:4*: "One thing I ask from the Lord, this is what I seek: that I may dwell in the house of the Lord all the days of my life, to gaze on the beauty of the Lord and to seek Him in His temple."

---

7 that is, of the Lord's Prayer.

(5) I appear with humility and fear before God, *Exodus* 28:17: "How holy is this place, this is nothing else than God's house, and this is the gate of heaven."

(6) That others may see my good works and praise the Father in heaven, *Matthew 5:16*. Since I cannot accomplish all of this by my own strength, I pray that God may guide me in all of these things.

(The Future of His Kingdom.)

39. What do you understand by God's Kingdom?

God's Kingdom is threefold: (1) The Kingdom of His power, (2) the Kingdom of His grace, and (3) the Kingdom of His glory. The first extends over all creatures, including the devils and condemned people. However, I pray that the Kingdom of grace and the Kingdom of glory may come to us.

40. How does the Kingdom of Grace come to us?

When God gives us His holy Word and Sacraments, offers us His fatherly love through them, comforts us with His promises of grace, and we accept them with faith and obedience; then His people will be joyful, despite the fact that, according to the world, they may experience tribulation. For the Kingdom of God is not about eating and drinking, but about righteousness, peace, and joy in the Holy Spirit, *Romans* 14:17.

41. What do you understand by the Kingdom of Glory?

Eternal blessedness, as stated in *Matthew 25:34*: "Come, you blessed of My Father, inherit the kingdom prepared for you from the foundation of the world." *1 Peter* 1:8: "You will rejoice with inexpressible and glorious joy." Thus, we pray that God may preserve us in this life with His grace, and after this life, make us partakers of the promised glory.

(Fulfillment of God's Will.)

42. What do you mean by the petition: "Your will be done, on earth as it is in heaven"?

God's will toward us humans is twofold: One is the will of the Law, which comes from His holy righteousness and governs all the works of men. Here, we pray that God may guide us in all our lives to do what pleases Him. *Psalm 143:10:* "Teach me to do Your will, for You are my God; Your good Spirit will lead me on level ground." In this way, the holy angels in heaven fulfill God's will and carry out His commands. *Psalm 103:20.*

43. Is it not also God's will that all sinners be condemned?

Indeed, it is. For St. Paul writes in *Romans 1:18:* "God's wrath is revealed from heaven against all ungodliness and unrighteousness of men." However, we pray that this wrathful will may not befall us. *Psalm 6:2:* "O Lord, rebuke me not in Your anger, nor chasten me in Your wrath." And *Psalm* 143:2: "Do not bring Your servant into judgment," etc.

44. What is the will of God for which we pray?

It is His gracious will, according to which He desires that we repent, remain in faith and holy living, be steadfast in His grace as long as we live in this world, and enjoy it in eternity. For it is His gracious will that all people be saved, *1 Timothy 2:4*, and that all turn to repentance, *2 Peter 3:9*. And all who believe in Christ shall not be lost but have eternal life, *John 3:16*. For this will, we implore Him in prayer.

(B. Bodily Necessities.[8])

45. Do you request all bodily goods in the fourth petition: "Give us this day our daily bread"?

Yes. St. Paul summed it up in two points: "If we have food and clothing, let us be content," *1 Timothy 6:8*. All of this comes from God: "The eyes of all look to You, Lord, and You give them their food at the proper time. You open Your hand and satisfy the desires of every living thing with favor," *Psalm 145:15–16*. Therefore, we pray that God, as a Father to His beloved children, may give us the necessary sustenance for the body.

---

8 Connecting back to the first point, at question 37.

46. Why do you call it daily bread, which God is to give us today?

This is said for two reasons: (1) So that we do not desire excess, but only what is necessary for us, which Solomon calls "the food that is convenient for me," *Proverbs 30:8*. And we pray that God may (according to His will) give us neither poverty nor riches. (2) So that I do not need to worry about the future, as the Lord says in *Proverbs 27:1*, but entrust this concern to God, *Matthew 6:34*, and trust Him, just as He prepares food for the birds each day, so will He not abandon me, but provide for my necessities.

47. What do you mean when you ask for "our bread"?

That I pray to God to protect us, so that neither I nor others obtain our bread and nourishment through deceit, false pretenses, or other dishonest means. Rather, I desire nothing more than what the Heavenly Father has provided and allotted to each person as their own. *Proverbs* 20:17, "Stolen bread tastes sweet to everyone, but afterward, their mouth will be full of gravel."

(C. Avoidance of Spiritual Harm.)

48. How many kinds of evil do you ask God to avert?

All of this is encompassed in the last three petitions, of which the fifth reads as follows: "Father, forgive us our debts, as we forgive our debtors."

(The Accusation of Sin.)

49. What do you understand by "debt"?

Since all people are obliged to obey God, *Luke 17:10*, every transgression and disobedience is a debt; therefore, the Lord Christ compares sins with debts, *Matthew 18*, *Luke 17*, and *St. Paul* writes in *Romans 3:19*, "Through the law, every mouth is silenced, so that the whole world is accountable to God."

50. Why do you pray for the remission of debts?

Because neither I nor any other person can make full satisfaction to God, the righteous Judge, for our sins, we must pray: "Lord, have mercy on us and cast all our sins into the depths of the sea," *Micah 7:18*, since His dear Son took them upon Himself, endured the punishment on our behalf, that we may have peace, *Isaiah 53*, and paid for what He did not steal, *Psalm 69:5*.

51. What does the phrase "as we forgive our debtors" mean?

It means that I must not pray to God with a false heart or in anger, *1 Timothy* 2:8, as the Lord Christ says: "If you do not forgive others their trespasses, neither will your Father forgive your trespasses." Therefore, I must diligently examine my heart before prayer, and if I find anger within, I must cast it out and willingly forgive anyone who has wronged me, so that my heavenly Father may also forgive my sins.

52. How? When anger had so taken over your heart that you could not forgive, no matter how much you would like to, must you therefore abandon the prayer entirely?

No. Rather, I must hate, subdue, and suppress the anger, and the prayer should be offered like this: "Dear Heavenly Father, out of grace forgive me my sins, and compel through Your Holy Spirit my sinful, evil disposition that always wants to keep hold of anger. Cleanse my heart from such disorder, so that I may approach Your presence with joyful courage and ask for forgiveness of my sins!"

(Evil Temptation.)

53. What is the other evil that you ask to be averted?

Temptation. For although God sometimes lays fatherly temptation upon people so that their faith, love for God, patience, and other virtues may be tested, to see whether they are righteous— such as the temptations that Abraham, Job, Tobias, and other saints faced and were found faithful—yet I ask that God would not allow me to fall into hostile temptation from the devil, the world, and my sinful flesh, or where my faith might also be inwardly attacked, so that I may overcome without harm to my soul.

54. Explain more clearly what is understood by the word "temptation."

Temptation is an inclination toward sin, by which a person may be cast into eternal harm and ruin of the soul. The devil tempted Judas when he put the thought in his mind to betray Christ, and when he put it in his mind to take his own life, *Mat. 27:5*. Both of these temptations were directed by the evil enemy. The world tempted Demas, causing him to abandon Paul and fall in love with this world, *2 Tim. 4:10*. The sinful flesh tempts us through its evil desires, which war against the soul, *1 Pet. 2:11*. Cain was tempted when, in his anger, he killed his brother, *Gen. 4:8*. David was tempted when he committed adultery with Bathsheba and killed Uriah, *2 Sam. 11:17*. Likewise, Satan tempted Peter through fear for his life, leading him to deny Christ, *Mat. 26:69*. When the devil prowls around me like a roaring lion, seeking to devour me, *1 Pet. 5:8*, and when the world and my sinful flesh actively assist him, I pray that God, as a faithful Father, will protect me so that I am not overcome and fall into God's wrath and eternal damnation, but instead strengthen me by His power so that I may resist all these temptations in faith and overcome them.

55. Can you not overcome these temptations yourself?

As little as a lamb can protect itself against a lion, so little can a person save themselves from the devil, since we are dead in sins, *Eph. 2:5*, and are not able to do anything properly, *John 15:5*. Therefore, the works of the devil are not destroyed by us, but only by Christ, *1 John 3:8*, and the desires of the flesh are abolished and put to death through the Holy Spirit, *Rom. 8:13*. Therefore, it is of great necessity that I ask God to protect me from harmful temptation, or at least to bring it to an end, so that I can endure it; *1 Cor. 10:13*.

(And all Misfortune.)

56. What is the third evil, from which you must ask God to avert?

The last petition encompasses all evils of both body and soul. Since I must go through this valley of tears, *Psalm 84:7*, and even when my life has been joyful, it has been nothing but toil and labor, *Psalm 90:11*, and pure misery from my mother's womb until I am laid in the earth, *Sirach 40:1*. Therefore, I must cast all my burdens upon the LORD, and if He lays a burden upon me, He will also help me powerfully, *Psalm 68:20*. Finally, He will lead me through much tribulation into His eternal and blessed kingdom, *Acts 14:22*.

3. In Thanksgiving.[9]

57. How do you serve God with thanksgiving?

His will and command is that when He helps me in response to my prayer, I should praise Him for it, *Psalm 50:15*. First and foremost, inwardly in the heart and soul, *Psalm 103:1*: "Bless the Lord, O my soul, and all that is within me, bless His holy name." However, since my thanksgiving for all spiritual and bodily blessings should demonstrate His love and praise toward my neighbor, I am obligated to give thanks to the Lord in the congregation and to praise Him in the entire assembly, *Psalm 22:23, 26*. And so that this may be done well, I must call upon God Himself, *Psalm 51:17*: "Open my lips, so that my mouth may declare Your praise."

4. In proper use of the Holy Sacraments.[10]

58. How should one rightly use the holy Sacraments?

Since there are two Sacraments—the Holy Baptism and the Lord's Supper—each is to be discussed individually.

(Holy Baptism.)

59. How can you make your Baptism useful to you?

Firstly, in faith: that I know through Holy Baptism I have become a partaker of the entire merit of Christ. *Romans 6:3*, "All of us who were baptized into Christ Jesus were baptized into His death; we were therefore buried with Him through baptism into

---

9 Referring back to the parts of the Divine Service in question 18.
10 Again, referring back to question 18.

death." *Galatians* 3:27, "For all of you who were baptized into Christ have clothed yourselves with Christ." (2) Through Baptism, God has established a covenant of grace with me. *1 Peter 3:21*, "Baptism is the pledge of a good conscience toward God." Therefore, God binds Himself to me, just as He did with Abraham, *Genesis 17:18*. Blessed is the God of truth; He will not abandon me in any need. (3) Through Holy Baptism, God has opened His heavenly kingdom to me, as Christ says in *John 3:5*, "Unless one is born of water and the Spirit, he cannot enter the kingdom of God." And He has given me eternal life. *Mark 16:16*, "Whoever believes and is baptized will be saved."

60. Does Holy Baptism also serve Christian life?

Yes, indeed. I should remember that Christ washed and cleansed me from sins in Baptism, *Ephesians 5:26*. Therefore, I should not, after this saving bath, roll again in the mud like a dog, as Saul did, *2 Peter 2:22*. Just as I have put on Christ as the garment of salvation and the robe of righteousness, *Isaiah 61:10*, I should not stain it with sins but rather walk in newness of life, *Romans 6:4*.

(The Holy Supper.)

61. How should I rightly use the Holy Supper?

Since St. Paul writes in *1 Corinthians* 11:28: "Let a man examine himself, and so let him eat of that bread and drink of that cup," I must examine myself in preparation for the Holy Supper before I partake, according to the Law and the Gospel.

62. How must one examine oneself according to the Law?

Firstly, whether I have sinned against God. For this purpose, the Law serves, from which comes the knowledge of sin, *Romans 3:20*.

Secondly, whether I deeply regret my sins, as Peter did *Matthew 26:75*, and as the sinful woman did, *Luke 7:38*, lamenting and sorrowfully repenting.

Thirdly, whether I so hate sin from the depths of my soul that I have resolutely committed to fleeing from it. If I find all of this in myself, then I have examined myself rightly according to the Law. But if there is any deficiency, I must reflect more deeply on God's Law, His wrath, and eternal damnation, and earnestly pray to God: "Turn me, and I shall be turned," *Jeremiah 31:18*.

63. Is all of this necessary for true repentance?

Yes, because: (1) If I do not recognize my sins, I do not seek the Savior. *Matthew 9:12*: "The healthy do not need a doctor, but the sick do." (2) If I do not repent of my sins, I am not truly desiring grace from the heart. (3) If I intend to continue living in sin, there is no good resolution within me, and the last state will be worse than the first, *2 Peter 2:20*.

64. How should one examine oneself according to the Gospel?

By examining: (1) Whether I have a heartfelt desire for the forgiveness of my sins, and whether I pray with David: "God, be gracious to me according to your goodness, and blot out my sin according to your great mercy," *Psalm 51:3*, and with the tax collector, "God, be merciful to me," *Luke 18:13*.

(2) Whether I am certain within myself that the Lord Christ has borne all my sins, *John 1:29*, and has paid for them on my behalf.

(3) Whether I truly find comfort in God's grace and in Christ's merit, and whether I have firm trust in God, that for Christ's sake, He forgives my sins.

65. Why is all this necessary?

Because: (1) If I have no hope for forgiveness, I would have to despair like Cain and Judas.

(2) If I doubt whether Christ has done enough for my sins, I also do not know if any grace from God could reach me.

(3) If I do not have such trust in God, I am without faith; but, without faith, it is impossible to please God, *Hebrews 11:6*.

66. How must I properly and as a Christian conduct myself when receiving the Holy Supper?

When I approach with a repentant and believing heart, as just indicated, I must: (1) Eat and drink.

(2) Stand firm on the word of truth, where Christ says: "Eat, this is My body, which is given for you." Likewise: "Drink, this is the new covenant in My blood, which is shed for you, for the forgiveness of sins," and be certain that the Lord Christ gives me, with the bread, His body to eat, and with the wine, His blood to drink.

(3) Do this in remembrance of Him; not as if I only remember His suffering and death as a historical event, but primarily to reflect that the Lord Jesus assures me with this pledge that He died for me, as explained above.

3. On Love for Neighbor.[11]

67. So far, we have spoken of love toward God; let us now also discuss love for our neighbor. How and in what does love for our neighbor consist?

God has shown this to us very clearly in *Leviticus 19:18*: "You shall love your neighbor as yourself." Christ has summed it up in this way: "Whatever you wish that others would do to you, do also to them." If I want to know how I should act toward my neighbor, I only need to consider how I would want others to treat me in every circumstance. In the same way, I must act toward others.

(What it is.)

68. Can you explain to me the second table of the Law piece by piece?

The second table of the Law is explained to me from the fourth commandment to the tenth. But before we get to that, I must carefully consider the last two commandments—the ninth and the tenth—as they also rebuke the desires of the heart and show that evil lust is sin.

(Of Evil Desires.)

69. What is this evil desire?

---

11 Continuing from point 2 on page 49.

This runs through all the commandments. Absalom desired to drive his father out of the kingdom, *2 Samuel 15:4*. Cain desired to kill his brother, *Genesis 4:5*. Likewise, Christ says: "Whoever looks at a woman with lust has already committed adultery with her in his heart," *Matthew 5:28*. Judas desired the thirty pieces of silver, *Matthew 26:15–16*. The adversaries of the prophet Jeremiah desired to kill him through slander with their tongues, *Jeremiah 18:18*.

70. Is, then, evil desire so harmful?

St. Peter says in *1 Peter 2:11*: "Abstain from fleshly lusts, which war against the soul." And just as I do not want others to have evil thoughts against me, so I must not have the same against others, lest I sin against my neighbor and bring myself into God's wrath and eternal damnation.

71. Which are the commandments that concern love for the neighbor?

The fourth and those that follow.

(Honor your superiors.)

72. What should I do according to the fourth commandment?

All those who are set before me as father and mother in the three estates, I should honor them with words, deeds, and patience.

(In the Teaching Office.)

73. Who are your Elders in the Teaching Office?

The Preachers and Instructors[12], who show me the way to salvation, through sound teaching, instruction, reproof, and warning. *2 Tim. 4:2*. And then through their good example, living a Christian life in love, in the Spirit, in faith, and in chastity, *1 Tim. 4:12*. These I should honor: (1) With obedience. *Heb. 13:17*: "Obey your Elders and submit to them, for they watch over your souls." (2) With works of love. *1 The. 5:12–13*: "We ask you, dear brothers, to recognize

---

12 *Die Prediger und Praeceptores*

those who labor among you, who are over you in the Lord and admonish you, and to esteem them very highly in love because of their work." (3) With generosity. *Gal.* 6:6: "Let the one who is taught the word share all good things with the one who teaches."

(In the Government Office.)

74. Who are your Elders in the Government Office?

All lawful secular authorities, who protect me with the sword, or external force, against evil people, forbid me from doing wrong, judge disputes, uphold justice, and punish evil. These I must honor: (1) with obedience and submission. *Rom.13:1:* "Let every person be subject to the governing authorities, for there is no authority except from God, and those that exist have been instituted by God." So we are subject out of necessity, not only for fear of punishment, but also for conscience's sake. (2) By providing necessary contributions for the government. *Rom.* 13:7: "Give to everyone what you owe them: taxes to whom taxes are owed, revenue to whom revenue is owed, respect to whom respect is owed, and honor to whom honor is owed." *Eccl.* 10:20: "Do not curse the king, even in your thoughts," etc.

(In the Household.)

75. Are those in the household my Elders to whom I owe obedience?

My Elders are those who raise me in the fear and admonition of the Lord, discipline me so that I may save my soul from hell, teach me all that is good by their example, instruct me, endure with me, etc. These are not only father and mother, but also guardians, masters and mistresses, patrons, and related friends, as well as others who take the place of father and mother and fulfill their role in my life.

76. How must I honor them?

(1) With sincere love; (2) With obedience, as the Child Jesus was subject to His parents, *Luke 2:51;* (3) With kind words and ges-

tures, as Joseph kissed his father, *Genesis 46:29*; (4) With patience, as Shem and Japheth patiently dealt with their drunken father, *Genesis 9:23.*

77. Does true obedience consist of doing everything that parents command?

When authorities, preachers, or others such as father and mother, command something that is contrary to God's Word and will, I must not do it, for we must obey God rather than men, *Acts 5:29.*

(Harm no one in body and life.)

78. How must I live according to the fifth commandment?

I must not inflict any harm on anyone's body, either by myself, as Cain killed Abel, *Genesis 4:8,* or through others, as David killed Uriah with the sword of the Ammonites, *2 Samuel 11:17.*

79. Is it wrong for the authorities to put evildoers to death?

When the authorities put to death those whom God has commanded to be killed, they act rightly as servants of God, who bear the sword as avengers to punish those who do evil, *Romans 13:4.* In doing so, they carry out God's judgment, which He has declared upon the wicked (*Exodus 6; Proverbs 8; Deuteronomy 22:22*), and other criminals.

80. If you do not kill anyone or harm their body, then have you kept this commandment?

No, for murder is also committed through anger and hatred, *1 John 3:15.* Whoever hates his brother is a murderer; with this, I not only harm my neighbor, but also my own body, *Sirach 30:26.* Jealousy and anger destroy life, even my soul. *Galatians 5:19, 20, 21:* "The works of the flesh are enmity, strife, jealousy, anger, quarrels, dissensions, of which I have told you before, and tell you again, that those who do such things will not inherit the Kingdom of God."

81. Is murder committed in other ways as well?

Yes. (1) Whoever can prevent murder, harm, anger, or hatred and does not do so, has committed murder. *Proverbs 24:11:* "Rescue those who are being taken away to death; hold back those who are stumbling to the slaughter." (2) Whoever rejoices or takes pleasure in murder or harm has made themselves guilty of another's murder, *2 Timothy 3:2.* Therefore, Solomon teaches *Proverbs 24:17–18:* "Do not rejoice when your enemy falls, and let not your heart be glad when he stumbles, lest the Lord see it and be displeased." (3) Whoever uses hostile words or gestures toward their neighbor is also a murderer. *Matthew 5:22:* "But I say to you that everyone who is angry with his brother will be liable to judgment; whoever insults his brother will be liable to the council; and whoever says, 'You fool!' will be liable to the hell of fire."

(Live chastely and modestly.)

82. What does the sixth commandment require?

It commands all chastity and forbids all unchastity, along with anything that leads to it. (1) Adultery. This occurs either when spouses leave each other, *Deuteronomy 19:12,* or engage in shameful acts with others, like David did with Uriah's wife, *2 Samuel 11:4.* (2) Fornication and improper lust, *Leviticus 34:2.* (3) All shameful words, foolish clothing, and jokes that are unbecoming of Christians, *Ephesians 5:4.* (4) Impure gestures and provocations. *Sirach 9:3–4:* "Flee from a loose woman, so that you do not fall into her nets; do not become accustomed to a songstress, lest she capture you with her enticements." (5) Light or seductive clothing, which caused Tamar to tempt Judah into fornication, *Genesis 38:14.* That is why such garments are called the adornment of a harlot, *Proverbs 5:10.* (6) Unchaste thoughts. *Matthew 5:28:* "Anyone who looks at a woman lustfully has already committed adultery with her in his heart."

(Do not harm anyone's goods.)

83. What kind of theft is forbidden in the seventh commandment?

(1) What is commonly called stealing, as when Judas was a thief and embezzled what was given to the Lord Christ, *John 12:6.*

(2) Violent robbery, where one forcibly takes what belongs to another.

(3) Excessive interest, through which someone is deprived of their possessions. *Exodus 22:25:* "If you lend money to My people, to the poor among you, do not act as a creditor to him by charging him interest."

(4) Taking unfair advantage of others in business dealings. *1 Thessalonians 4:6:* "That no one should wrong or take advantage of a brother or sister in this matter, for the Lord is the avenger of all such offenses."

(5) Neglect of almsgiving, which everyone is required to give to the poor from their goods. *Luke 6:38:* "Give, and it will be given to you."

(6) The squandering of one's goods through excessive feasting, gambling, laziness, extravagant clothing, etc., by which one deprives oneself and one's family of what is theirs. *Proverbs 23:21:* "For drunkards and gluttons become poor, and drowsiness clothes them in rags."

(Nor harm their honor and good name.)

84. What is included in the eighth commandment?

All words that harm one's neighbor.

(1) When one speaks falsely against a companion; false teachers pretend to be apostles of Christ and lead people to hell, *Matthew 23:15.*

(2) When one speaks falsely against someone's innocence, with lies; for example, when priests were innocently killed. *1 Samuel 22:9.*

(3) When one speaks falsely against another's honor, as Potiphar's wife slandered Joseph, accusing him of attempting to violate her, *Genesis 39:14.*

(4) When someone speaks falsely against another's possessions. Ziba deceived Mephibosheth, so that David took half of his possessions and gave them to Ziba, *2 Samuel 16:3–4.*

(5) When sworn oaths are broken.

(6) When false testimony is given in court.

(7) When someone unjustly speaks ill of their neighbor.

(8) When someone harbors false suspicions.

(9) When someone interprets another's words or actions in a negative way. *Sirach* 6:5: "Whoever interprets everything in the best way, makes many friends."

85. When you take all of this into diligent consideration, have you then kept God's Law?

When I diligently examine myself without hypocrisy, I find that there is always a shortcoming. If not in knowledge, then in words, deeds, and thoughts, I do not fully accomplish the good. *Romans 7:18.* However, I must strive for perfection, if I may attain it. *Philippians 3:12.* And I must continually strengthen myself in Christianity from one moment to the next, until I become perfect in the life to come.

Dearest God and Father! Since I was conceived and born in sin, and by nature am so utterly corrupt that my thoughts and desires are only evil continually, and my perverse heart always chooses the wrong paths, teach me, Lord, what is beneficial, and guide me in the way that I should go. Teach me to do what pleases You, for You are my God. May Your good Spirit lead me on level ground, so that I may walk the narrow path to life with purity and without stumbling, enter through the narrow gate to life, and rejoice with You forever, for the sake of my Lord Jesus Christ, who is the way to You and to Your eternal kingdom. Amen.

THE THIRD PART.—PREPARATION FOR BLESSED DYING.

1. In what does the wholesome preparation for a blessed death consist?

It consists of five main points. That I diligently pay attention:

(1) To myself.

(2) To God, in whose hands my life and death rest.

(3) To Christ, who is my life.

(4) To my neighbors, with and among whom I live and have lived in this world.

(5) To my return to those things in which I have formerly inclined or strayed from God, that in all these things, I set no stumbling block, but rather promote my salvation in all respects.

1. In reflection on oneself.

2. How must I pay attention to myself?

Thus, so that while I am still in good and healthy days:

(1) Whether I am young or old, I remember my death: "You are dust, and to dust you shall return," *Genesis 3:19.* Therefore, I should never let the thought of death leave my mind.

(2) I diligently recognize that I must be prepared for death every day and hour, and not live like the animals, thinking that I will never die, *Ecclesiastes 9:12:* "For man does not know his time; like fish that are caught in an evil net, and like birds that are trapped in a snare, so too are men ensnared in a time of disaster when it suddenly falls upon them." Therefore, a man must always be ready for death, for you do not know at what hour your Lord will come, *Matthew 24:42.*

(3) I also remind myself constantly; since through death I enter into eternity, and it is appointed for man once to die, and after that the judgment, *Hebrews 9:27.* That I expect such a judgment as I will be found in death. *Ecclesiastes11:3:* "If the tree falls toward the south or toward the north, wherever it falls, there it will lie."

3. How do you use this to your benefit?

(1) I follow the apostolic admonition: "Walk carefully, as the wise," *Ephesians 5:15.*

(2) I live constantly as though I must die every day; I do not boast about tomorrow, for I do not know what the day may bring, *Proverbs 27:1.*

(3) Thus, I ensure that nothing in my works, words, or thoughts would bring regret in my final hour or when I appear before God's judgment; for whatever I do, I consider the end, so that I may never do evil, *Sirach 7:36.* Therefore, Solomon teaches me, *Ecclesiastes 11:9:* "Rejoice, O young man, in your youth, and let your heart be glad in the days of your youth, and follow the desires of your heart—but know that for all these things God will bring you into judgment."

(4) I guard myself with great diligence against all sins. For I know that I can neither justify evil deeds, nor evil words or thoughts before God's judgment. Therefore, I apply all my heart and strength to this, and take to heart the warning of *Sirach 21:2–4:* "Flee from sin as from a serpent, for if you come too close, it will bite you; its teeth are like lion's teeth and they will kill a person. Every sin is like a sharp sword and wounds, which no one can heal."

(5) As for the sins I have committed, even if I am not aware of all of them, I daily ask God for forgiveness. Heavenly Father, forgive me my sins, *Matthew 6:12.* Forgive me also my hidden faults, *Psalm 19:13.*

(6) I take no pleasure in the sins of others nor do I approve of them, so that I do not become a participant in the sins of others, *1 Timothy 5:22.*

2. God.

4. How do you prepare yourself for a blessed departure by contemplating and reflecting on God?

Here I must carefully consider that God deals with people according to either justice or mercy. Regarding justice:

(1) When He allows people to die because of their sins, *Psalm 90:4*: "Lord, You cause men to die." *Job 14:5*: "You have set a limit for man, and he will not go beyond it."

(2) When He sets the stiff-necked godless ones in slippery places and casts them down to the ground so that they suddenly come to nothing, perish, and meet a dreadful end. *Psalm 73:18–19*.

(3) When He kills them and sends them to burn in hell: Then remains a fearful expectation of judgment and of fiery wrath that will consume the godless, *Hebrews 10:26*.

5. How can you make use of this?

In this way:

(1) That I do not think I will die by chance, *Wisdom 2:2*, but rather according to God's will, who has also spoken over me because of sin: "You are dust, and to dust you shall return," *Genesis 3:19*. For death is the wages of sin, *Romans 6:23*. Through one man, sin entered the world, and death through sin, and so death spread to all people because all have sinned, *Romans 5:12*. Therefore, I must resign myself to this reality and accept my soul with patience, *Luke 21:19*.

(2) That I do not live securely in sin and wander carelessly through life, as if I were not going to die. Thus David prays: "Lord, teach me that my end must come, and that my life has a limit, and that I must depart," *Psalm 39:4*. Make us mindful that we must die, so that we may become wise.

(3) That I do not act wickedly against my God, as Solomon warns, *Ecclesiastes 7:18*: "Do not be overly wicked, and do not be foolish; why should you die before your time?" *2 Samuel 3:18*. And I fear Him as the only Judge, *Matthew 10:28*: "Fear Him who can destroy both body and soul in hell."

(4) That I honor my God throughout my life, serve Him, and obey Him, *Ecclesiastes 12:13–14*: "Fear God and keep His commandments, for this is the duty of all mankind." For God will bring every work into judgment, whether hidden, good, or evil. And I tremble at the thought of falling into the hands of the living God, *Hebrews 10:31*.

(5) That I earnestly ask God for forgiveness for how I have sinned against Him; *Psalm 51:3:* "God, be merciful to me according to Your kindness, and blot out my sins according to Your great mercy."

(6) That I do not set my heart on the world, but only concern myself with how I may avert God's righteous anger. *Matthew 16:26:* "What does it profit a man if he gains the whole world but loses his soul?"

6. How does God deal with us humans according to His mercy?

(1) When He does not leave me in my sins under His wrath, but has patience with me and does not wish for anyone to be lost, but that everyone would come to repentance, *2 Peter 3:9.* And thus leads us to repentance through His goodness, *Romans 2:4.*

(2) When He gives the Comforter, the Holy Spirit, to those who love and fear Him in their final hour, who reminds them of everything He has taught them through the Word, *John 14:26.* The Spirit bears witness with their spirit that they are God's children, *Romans 8:16,* and serves as a pledge of their inheritance, that they may know the riches of His glorious inheritance among His saints, *Ephesians 1:14, 18.*

(3) When He allows them to depart from this life in peace, gently and blessedly into eternal life, *Luke 2:29.*

(4) When He commands His angels to carry the souls of the departed into Abraham's bosom, *Luke 16:22.*

(5) When He leads them through death into life. *John 5:24:* "Truly, truly, I say to you: Whoever hears My word and believes in Him who sent Me has eternal life, and does not come into judgment, but has passed from death to life."

(6) When He finally grants them joy after their suffering, according to His promise. *Isaiah 25:8:* "The Lord will wipe away the tears from all faces." *Isaiah 35:10:* "Everlasting joy will be upon their heads; they will obtain gladness and joy, and sorrow and sighing will flee away."

(7) When He will raise them from the dead to eternal life. *John 5:28–29:* "The hour is coming in which all who are in the graves will hear the voice of the Son of Man and come forth—those who

have done good, to the resurrection of life."

7. What is the purpose of this testimony?

(1) That I give heartfelt thanks to God for His unspeakable grace, and pray without ceasing that He may preserve me in the same [grace] until my blessed end, and never turn away from me, as He has promised. *Isaiah 54:10:* "'For the mountains may depart and the hills be removed, but my steadfast love shall not depart from you, and my covenant of peace shall not be removed,' says the Lord, your compassionate one."

(2) That I turn to God daily and not go from one time to another in impenitence. *Sirach 18:22*, "Do not delay your repentance until the grave, but amend your ways while you can still sin, and do not wait to better your life until death." *Psalm 95:8*, "Today, if you hear the Lord's voice, do not harden your hearts."

(3) That I ask for the comfort and assistance of the Holy Spirit. *Psalm 51:14*, "Comfort me with your help, and let the joyful Spirit sustain me." *Psalm 143:10*, "Let your good Spirit lead me on level ground, and let me be mightily comforted by this assistance, as a pledge of my inheritance." *Ephesians 1:14.*

(4) That I do not fear death, but rather rejoice in it because of the promised salvation. *Psalm 27:14*, "I believe that I shall see the goodness of the Lord in the land of the living." *Psalm 42:3*, "When shall I come and appear before God?" *Philippians 1:23*, "I desire to depart and to be with Christ, which is far better, and yet my soul remains still." "Be confident and at peace; I will walk before the Lord in the land of the living," *Psalm 116:7–9.*

3. Of the Lord Christ.

8. Thirdly, what must you take into consideration about Christ when contemplating death?

Many significant points.

(1) I look to Christ as the One who came to destroy the works of Satan, *1 John 3:8*. Among which, not the least, is that through the envy of the devil, death entered into the world, *Wisdom*

2:24. But Christ has become the poison of death, *Hosea 13:14*. He has taken away the power of death, *2 Timothy 1:10*. Thus, for all believing Christians, death is no longer death, but rather a passage from this miserable life to a blessed life, *John 5:24*: "Whoever hears My word and believes in Him who sent Me has eternal life and will not come into judgment, but has passed from death to life."

(2) Thus, Christ's work of grace, as He has conquered death, *Revelation 1:18*, will also raise me from the dead on the Last Day, granting me an immortal body, *John 6:40*: "This is the will of Him who sent Me: that everyone who sees the Son and believes in Him shall have eternal life, and I will raise him up on the Last Day."

(3) Since hell follows after death, *Revelation 6:8*, in order that death does not lead me to hell, Christ has become a plague to hell, *Hosea 13:14*. And by the blood of His covenant, He has freed the prisoners from the pit where there is no water, *Zechariah 9:11*.

(4) And this is because Christ the Lord faithfully helps me before God's judgment, as He, through His suffering and death: 1. has taken away the power of the devil, *Hebrews 2:14*, who accuses me before God day and night, *Revelation 12:10*; 2. has atoned for my sins, by taking upon Himself the punishment, that I might have peace, *Isaiah 53:5–6*. Of this, Paul writes in *Colossians 2:14*, "He has forgiven us all our sins and erased the record of debt that stood against us, removing it from our midst and nailing it to the cross." 3. *2 Corinthians 5:19*, God was in Christ and reconciled the world to Himself and did not count their sins against them. 4. He has redeemed me from the coming wrath, *1 Thessalonians 1:10*. 5. After He ascended into heaven, He sat down at the right hand of God, became my advocate and intercessor, and intercedes for me, *Romans 8:34*. Therefore, St. John also directs me to Him, *1 John 2:1*, "If anyone sins, we have an advocate with the Father, Jesus Christ, the Righteous One."

9. How does this benefit you and lead to salvation?

Through faith, or the heartfelt trust I place in my Savior. When I:

(1) Recognize that Christ endured such great suffering for

the sake of all mankind, and therefore also for my sake, and obtained for me eternal redemption, *Hebrews 9:12*.

(2) When I also gratefully and with a reverent heart accept that Christ has paid my debt, reconciled me to the Father, and restored life and true righteousness to me, *Daniel 9:24*.

(3) Remain of good cheer, also trusting in my gracious God and Redeemer that He will keep the precious inheritance He has purchased for me until that day, *2 Timothy 1:12*, and thus He will bring to completion the good work He has begun in me for my salvation, *Philippians 1:6*.

Thus, I am grafted into Christ through faith, *Romans 11:23*. Christ dwells through faith in my heart, *Ephesians 3:17*, and I am a Christian, and thus made partaker of His righteousness, life, and salvation, *Hebrews 3:14*. Therefore, there is no condemnation for all those who are in Christ Jesus, including me, *Romans 8:1*. He has been made unto me by God as wisdom, righteousness, sanctification, and redemption, *1 Cor. 1:30*.

4. Concerning Your Neighbor.

10. How do you prepare yourself for a blessed death by looking after your neighbor?

In this regard, my neighbors are the members of my household and those who are my flesh and blood. I ensure that (1) I raise them in the fear and admonition of the Lord, *Ephesians 6:4*, that they live in godliness, which holds the promise of this life and the life to come, *1 Timothy 4:8*. Additionally, (2) I ensure they learn something good, so that they are found in a state of good works, and wherever there is a need for them, they are not unfruitful, *Titus 3:14*. Then, (3) as much as God grants me through honorable means, I provide for their needs, *1 Timothy 5:8*. Once I am separated from them, I no longer need to worry about them, for I leave behind the One who can help them against their enemies, *Sirach 30:5–6*. Finally, (5) I entrust them to God's protection and grace, who is a father to the orphans and a defender of widows, *Psalm 68:6*.

5. Concerning Enemies.

11. How must you conduct yourself toward your enemies?

In this way: (1) I take great care to ensure that I do not fall into enmity with anyone. If it happens, I do not let the sun go down on my anger, *Ephesians 4:26*. Before I go to my resting place, I go and reconcile with my adversary and make peace while I am still on the way with him, *Matthew 5:25*. I consider the end and let go of the enmity that seeks death and destruction, *Sirach 28:6–7*. I remember that enmity, anger, quarrels, and hatred are works of the flesh, of which St. Paul has said before, those who do such things will not inherit the kingdom of God, *Galatians 5:12*. I remind myself of Christ's word, *Luke 6:37*: "Forgive, and you will be forgiven." I look to His example, that He prayed for His enemies, *Luke 23:34*, and I follow Him all the more willingly, knowing that through much tribulation, I must enter the kingdom of God, *Acts 14:22*.

If another person is angry with me, and I am aware of it, I gently rebuke them for their wrongdoing, so that they may come to the recognition of their sin and seek reconciliation. *Matthew 18:15*. However, I keep a free, untroubled heart and conscience, so that at any time, even if God calls me from this world through death, I am ready.

12. How must one conduct oneself in sickness, and when the end draws near, in a Christian manner?

I must prepare myself accordingly, since I see that many die suddenly, even before they fall ill, without having the chance to prepare for a blessed death, as they thought they would have enough time when they became sick. For man does not know his time; like fish caught in a net or birds trapped, not expecting it, so, too, are men ensnared at an evil time when it suddenly befalls them, *Ecclesiastes 9:12*. Therefore, I must also be watchful, expecting the last day at every moment, as it will come like a thief in the night when people say, "Peace, there is no danger," and then sudden destruction will come upon them, as St. Paul teaches us in *1 Thessalonians 5:1–3*. Consequently, I must always prepare my heart for this and for the final judgment, so that when the Lord comes, I will be found ready.

Practical Guidance in Sickness and at the End of Life.

13. If God were to allow me to come to my sickbed and face death, how should I conduct myself then?

As I have prepared myself for death during healthy days according to the instruction given thus far, I must remain in such readiness until my last breath. And,

(1) I must take refuge in the gracious and merciful Lord, the Lord who delivers from death, *Psalm 68:21*. I cast all my cares upon Him, *1 Pet. 5:7*, and trust in Him. Whether it leads to life or death, He will make it well, *Psalm 37:5*.

(2) I must, according to Sirach's teaching, cease from sin, make my hands unstained, and cleanse my heart from all iniquity, *Sirach 38:10*. And I must unceasingly pray for the forgiveness of my sins: "God, be merciful to me, a sinner!" *Luke 18:13*. "O Lord, do not remember the sins of my youth, nor my transgressions; but remember me according to Your great mercy and for the sake of Your goodness." *Psalm 25:7*.

(3) Afterward, I must set my earnest longing toward God and, like St. Paul, sigh: "I have a desire to depart and be with Christ," *Philippians 1:23*. And with holy Jacob: "Lord, I wait for your salvation." *Genesis 49:18*.

(4) Then I should set my house in order, draft my last will in a testament while in sound mind, so that after my departure there will be no quarrels among the heirs, whether the inheritance is little or much. In doing so, I should not forget the poor and those who work in churches and schools.

(5) After this, I must forget all earthly things, direct my soul and all thoughts toward God, and through devout confession, cleanse my heart of all misdeeds, *Sirach 38:10*. By the wholesome use of the Holy Sacrament, I nourish my soul with the blessed food and drink of the body and blood of Jesus Christ as a sure pledge that He has loved me, given Himself for me, and cleansed me from sin with His precious blood. Thus, I am assured of His steadfast grace, and I can more joyfully await my hour of death.

(6) I must cling to my Lord Jesus with all my heart, cast aside all sorrow, and, as my only comfort and Savior, ask Him with full hope and firm trust for forgiveness and justification. Along with the whole of Christendom, I say: "Yes, come, Lord Jesus!," *Revelation 22:20.* Following Job's example: "I know that my Redeemer lives, and He will raise me up from the earth after this," *Job 19:25.*

(7) And I must pray for the Holy Spirit's assistance, that He may fill my heart with complete hope and abundant comfort so that I may face death with courage, *Proverbs 14:32.*

(8) I must commend my soul to my God, the faithful Creator, *1 Peter 4:19,* speaking with the Lord Jesus, "Father, into Your hands I commit my spirit," *Luke 23:46.* Likewise, I entrust my soul into the loving hands of my Redeemer, sighing with David: "Into Your hands I commit my spirit; You have redeemed me, O Lord, faithful God," *Psalm 31:5.* And with Stephen: "Lord Jesus, receive my spirit!," *Acts 7:59.* Thus, my end will be as gentle as any other, for I will depart peacefully and blessedly into Your hands, Jesus! There, in Your hands, I shall rest gently and well in Abraham's bosom until the resurrection, when the body will no longer leave Your hands—with inexpressible and glorious joy.

Help, Lord Jesus Christ, through Your bitter suffering and death, through Your divine blood and Your five red wounds, that we may learn all this beneficially, practice it well and successfully, and rejoice in Your eternal and blessed kingdom without end, giving You praise, honor, glory, and thanks from eternity to eternity. Amen.

END

www.ingramcontent.com/pod-product-compliance
Lightning Source LLC
Chambersburg PA
CBHW070837050426
42452CB00011B/2319